PEACEMAKERS

OTHER BOOKS BY DOUGLAS ROCHE

The Catholic Revolution (McKay, 1968)

Man to Man (with Bishop Remi De Roo, Bruce, 1969)

It's A New World (Western Catholic Reporter, 1970)

Justice Not Charity: A New Global Ethic for Canada (McClelland and Stewart Ltd., 1976)

The Human Side of Politics (Clarke, Irwin, 1976)

What Development Is All About: China, Indonesia, Bangladesh (NC Press, 1979)

Politicians for Peace (NC Press, 1983)

United Nations: Divided World (NC Press, 1984)

Building Global Security: Agenda for the 1990's (NC Press, 1989)

In the Eye of the Catholic Storm (with Bishop Remi De Roo and Mary Jo Leddy, HarperCollins 1992)

A Bargain for Humanity: Global Security By 2000 (University of Alberta Press, 1993)

Safe Passage into the Twenty-First Century: The United Nations Quest for Peace, Equality, Justice and Development (with Robert Muller Continuum, 1995)

An Unacceptable Risk: Nuclear Weapons in a Volatile World (Project Ploughshares, 1995)

The Ultimate Evil: The Fight to Ban Nuclear Weapons (Lorimer, 1997)

Bread Not Bombs: A Political Agenda for Social Justice (University of Alberta Press, 1999)

The Human Right to Peace (Novalis, 2003)

Beyond Hiroshima (Novalis, 2005)

Global Conscience (Novalis, 2007)

Creative Dissent: A Politician's Struggle for Peace (Novalis, 2008)

How We Stopped Loving the Bomb (Lorimer, 2011)

PEACEMAKERS

HOW PEOPLE AROUND THE WORLD ARE BUILDING
A WORLD FREE OF WAR

DOUGLAS ROCHE

James Lorimer & Company Ltd., Publishers
Toronto

James Lorimer & Company Ltd., Publishers acknowledges the support of the Ontario Arts Council. We acknowledge the financial support of the Government of Canada through the Canada Book Fund for our publishing activities. We acknowledge the support of the Canada Council for the Arts which last year invested $24.3 million in writing and publishing throughout Canada. We acknowledge the Government of Ontario through the Ontario Media Development Corporation's Ontario Book Initiative.

Cover design: Meghan Collins
Cover image: Shutterstock

Library and Archives Canada Cataloguing in Publication

Roche, Douglas, 1929-, author
  Peacemakers : how people around the world are building a world free of war.

Includes bibliographical references and index.
ISBN 978-1-4594-0623-0 (pbk.).--ISBN 978-1-4594-0628-5 (epub)

  1. Pacifists--Biography. 2. Pacific settlement of international disputes. 3. Peace. I. Title.

JZ5540.R63 2014   327.1'720922   C2013-907733-2

James Lorimer & Company Ltd., Publishers
317 Adelaide Street West, Suite 1002
Toronto, ON, Canada
M5V 1P9
www.lorimer.ca

Printed and bound in Canada.

Peace to the 360,000 children who will be born across the world on the day this book is published.

"I have no doubt that forty years from now we shall . . . be engaged in the same pursuit. How could we expect otherwise? World organization is still a new adventure in human history. It needs much perfecting in the crucible of experience and there is no substitute for time in that respect."

— Dag Hammarskjöld, address at New York University, May 20, 1956

CONTENTS

INTRODUCTION:
Breaking Free From the Bonds of War

The world is moving to a more peaceful state. If you look at the headlines of the day, that statement might seem wishful thinking, but it is true. Today more people than at any other time in history are able to pursue, as the Universal Declaration of Human Rights puts it, their "right to life, liberty and security of person." I am not saying that we are living in harmony, that violence is ended, that suffering is eliminated. I am saying that more people are freed from the physical acts of warfare than ever before. We have not arrived at a destination called "peace," but our journey toward that destination is picking up speed. Recognizing the journey we are on gives us hope for a future of more peaceful conditions. That is what this book is about.

Two experiences prompted me to write the book. The first, a three-week global tour in 2011, convinced me that the world is moving into a new stage in the long quest to eliminate nuclear weapons. On that trip I brought a brief from the Middle Powers Initiative, a civil society organization dedicated to nuclear disarmament (which I chaired for many years), to senior government officials in China, India, Russia, the United Kingdom, and several European countries. The ideology that drove the escalation of nuclear weapons in the Cold War is long gone; younger officials are coming into status positions; and pragmatists are looking to maintain security without spending the $100 billion a year now devoured by the nuclear weapons industry for weapons whose use has been ruled out on political, military and moral grounds. In the discussions surrounding my lectures to university students, think tanks, and civil society groups it became clear that the intellectual case for nuclear deterrence is crumbling. All governments make excuses for resisting collaborative efforts to negotiate a global ban on nuclear weapons, but the ideas behind the anti–nuclear weapons campaign are beginning to take hold.

In 2012, I was in New York when Hurricane Sandy struck the Atlantic Seaboard. This is the second experience that prompted this book. I was stunned by what I saw in that city. Total gridlock on the streets. A quarter of the city without power for five days. Subways, bridges, tunnels, and airports closed. Schools and businesses shut down. Whole areas flooded. Hundreds of homes on fire. Hospitals evacuated. Four-hour line-ups just to get on a bus or buy gas. And, of course, many people killed. It was instantly clear that big cities are increasingly vulnerable to weather extremes and cannot cope with massive disruption. How would any city cope with a nuclear bomb explosion? A bigger question is behind such a spectre: Why should modern, globalized civilization tolerate the twin threats of climate change and nuclear weapons when we have the technology and political mechanisms to avert catastrophes?

The world is moving ahead in its thinking and yet we live on the edge of disaster. We are resisting a full political and financial commitment to the mechanisms for peace because we don't know enough about those mechanisms and certainly lack confidence in them. We need greater courage to take the leap to a successful world in which violence, mass poverty, and discrimination would be blights of the past.

By "peace" I do not mean a state of utopia. Rather, I take my cue from Dag Hammarskjöld, greatest of all UN secretaries-general, who defined peace in a way that greatly appeals to me: "Peace is not just the passive state of affairs in a world without war. It is a state of living devoted to action in order to build a world of prosperity and equity where occasions for conflicts either disappear or are quickly challenged if they arise." *Peace is a state of living devoted to action*: I like this core thought. All people have a right to actively pursue the full implementation of their human dignity free from war. More and more across the world, "peacemakers" are doing just that.

There is a very strong base on which to project a more hopeful future. A new global civilization is emerging. The advances in science, medicine, technology, communications, and travel have raised standards of living everywhere. Between 1990 and 2010, two billion people gained access to improved drinking water sources, such as piped supplies and protected wells. Rates of child mortality have fallen in all regions of the world in the last two decades — down by at least half in much of Asia, northern Africa, Latin America, and the Caribbean. More women are literate and educated than ever before, and the education gap with men has shrunk dramatically. A new middle class is rising in Asia. Sub-Saharan Africa is shaking off endemic poverty. The evidence of the decline of violence is piling up. Across the world, people want peace not war. There has never been a more propitious time to move forward in establishing a culture of peace that will lead, in time, to enshrining the right to peace.

First, we must deal with the contradictions that confuse many people, not least political decision makers. Anxiety for our security is a hallmark of our age. Every day brings new accounts of violence, war, famine, ecological disaster, and political turmoil. When I tell my friends that the incidence of physical violence across the world is actually trending down, they look at me querulously. Yet the *Human Security Report* of 2010, published by Simon Fraser University's School for International Studies, reported that high-intensity wars, those that kill at least one thousand people a year, have declined by 78 per cent since 1988. Even the upsurge of violence and the use of chemical weapons in Syria in 2013, tragic as it was, does not change the global downward trend. People are inundated with ghastly images of brutality brought to them by round-the-clock reporting of existing conflicts. But it is the scale of the reporting that has intensified, not the total acts of violence itself.

It is estimated that about one hundred million people were killed in the wars of the twentieth century. Today, there are virtually no wars between states. In the first decade of this century, 131 warlords, dictators, and the like, who had caused mass carnage were convicted of crimes against humanity in tribunals that never existed before. Fewer people today are arbitrarily killed and tortured by their own government; there are fewer civil wars and they tend to be shorter.

UN peacekeeping, currently deploying more than one hundred thousand troops on sixteen missions, is at an all-time high. Since its inception in 1997, the Anti-Personnel Mine Ban Convention (the treaty banning landmines) has saved countless lives. The new Arms Trade Treaty, though far from perfect, will now regulate the $70 billion annual arms business. World military expenditures are slightly decreasing. Three-quarters of the world's nations have voted at the UN to commence negotiations to ban all nuclear weapons.

Of course, wars have not ended and there is no guarantee of peace. The world is still spending $1.7 trillion a year on arms, and the continued existence of seventeen thousand nuclear weapons with the power to cause unimaginable catastrophe is a sobering reminder of the precariousness of peace. But it would be irresponsible to close our eyes to the effects of the peace-building programs found around the world.

Consider some of the places whose very names conjure the spectre of genocide and mass human suffering in the recent past: Rwanda, Bosnia, Cambodia, Hiroshima, Northern Ireland. In the small East African nation of Rwanda, where about eight hundred thousand people were killed over the span of a hundred days in 1994, commerce is beginning to thrive in a stable atmosphere. In Bosnia, where thousands of Muslims were massacred in the worst crime on European soil since the Second World War, now Muslims and Serbs live in a fragile peace. In Cambodia, where two million people died in the "killing fields," the international community mounted an effective restoration program, and the country has become a tourist centre of South Asia. In Hiroshima, where the first atomic bomb to be used in war killed 140,000 people, the rebuilt, vigorous city is a centre of the anti–nuclear weapons campaign. In Northern Ireland, "the Troubles" — the fierce and violent clashes between Catholics and Protestants in which 3,500 people were slain — had been seen as one of the world's intractable conflicts, but today the people live basically in peace.

The list of war-torn places that have given way to processes of peace and reconciliation is long: Angola, Ivory Coast, Mozambique, Guatemala, El Salvador, East Timor, Sierra Leone. All these places have stories to tell of building the conditions for peace. New mechanisms to improve peacekeeping, peace-building, and international justice, many under United Nations auspices, are laboriously being built. This creativity goes largely unreported, and people are unaware of the great strides being made in changing the old culture of war into a culture of peace. Despite the headlines, a new dynamic for peace exists in the world. As former US president Bill Clinton noted: "In places once synonymous with conflict, like the Balkans and Rwanda, former antagonists are now working together to solve problems."

We agonize over the one hundred thousand deaths so far in the Syrian conflict and criticize the decades-long Israel-Palestine impasse. We are preoccupied by zones of conflict and the seeming inability of the international community to bring combatants to the peace table. But we must not lose sight that the world as a whole — including huge areas of Africa, Asia, and Latin America — is entering the most hopeful state of peace in human history. There is no better example of how the world is moving from war to peace than Europe, which suffered through two world wars in the twentieth century and now basks in the glow of the 2012 Nobel Peace Prize, awarded to the European Union, for having advanced peace and reconciliation, democracy and human rights over six decades in Europe.

When the Obama administration tried to drum up support for a military intervention in Syria, it was resoundingly rebuffed around the world, including by the American public. Yet ten years earlier, President Bush held Western public opinion on his side when the US invaded Iraq. Within a decade, public opinion shifted against war and for the UN Security Council to do its job of finding a diplomatic solution to the Syrian uprising. The international aversion to NATO going to war in Syria was palpable. In fact, NATO's supreme commander General Jean-Paul Palomeros has publicly complained that the biggest "threat" facing the alliance is the massive reduction in defence spending of its members.

People were lied to in the prosecution of the Iraq and Afghanistan wars and the Vietnam war before that. The consequent distrust of political leaders is one reason for today's scepticism towards the need for war. But the reasons for the growing rejection of war lie deeper. Gradually, humanity is beginning to understand that war is futile. That is a huge gain in the struggle for peace. The public rejection of war has enormous ramifications for how society will conduct its affairs. It portends an upswing in acceptance of the role of the UN as a mediating force.

New thinking for the protection and development of the human community is taking form. It is a moment of astonishing change in the history of the world. The Arab Spring, the Occupy movement, the marches against war are only the opening notes. Humanity is discovering a power it never had before to construct a more peaceful world.

To get a wider outlook than just my own, I conducted sixty interviews with leaders in many fields for this book. Here you will meet former prime ministers, former foreign ministers, Nobel Peace Prize laureates, a prince, senior UN officials, ambassadors, outstanding women, leading religious figures, authors, journalists, jurists, and civil society activists. All of them enriched my understanding of how the world is moving against war. Every one of them not only believes peace is possible but is working to achieve it.

CHAPTER 1:
Fewer Arms, Less Conflict

It was the Wednesday afternoon of the final week of the United Nations Conference on the Arms Trade Treaty in March 2013. Ambassador Peter Woolcott — the fifty-nine-year-old Australian diplomat presiding over the 180 countries gathered in the North Lawn Building of the United Nations in New York — thought he still had a chance to win consensus in the negotiations. A seven-year effort to regulate the international trade in conventional arms — from small arms to battle tanks, combat aircraft, and warships — had produced a draft treaty which, though far from perfect, set new international standards for regulating the $70 billion business that fuels conflict, undermines peace and security, threatens economic and social development, and causes widespread human suffering. "I thought we still had a chance for consensus, which was always going to be extremely hard," Woolcott told me in an interview, "but in our consultation, the Iranian delegate told me Tehran had given instructions to block it."

At a formal meeting the next morning Iran protested that the treaty exempted the transfer of arms for armed forces of countries outside their territories and that these had been used in the Middle East and the Persian Gulf, a not-too-subtle jab at the US for its war in Iraq. North Korea and Syria then raised their nameplates to claim the floor to voice objections. Woolcott said the conference's inability to agree was disappointing but, unflinching, he told the delegates, "the treaty is coming." He gave the floor to Kenya, which proposed sending the draft to the floor of the UN General Assembly for a vote.

As a first order of business the following week, the General Assembly voted 155 in favour of adopting the treaty with three votes against and twenty-two abstaining. Thus what was denied consensus passage in the conference was obtained by majority vote in the General Assembly. Many governments and civil society members hailed the achievement as the first-ever global treaty to establish common standards for regulating the international trade in conventional arms, and thus a major step forward in international law. UN Secretary-General Ban Ki-moon, praising Woolcott's "open and transparent manner," said the new treaty "will help to keep warlords, pirates, terrorists, criminals and their like from acquiring deadly arms." It will likely take a year or two for the requisite fifty countries to ratify it before the treaty comes into effect.

Woolcott's steering of the process through the hard-line shoals of Iran on the one side and the United States on the other, as well as the quality of the end product tell us a lot about the fragile state of international relations today, how hard it is to establish substantive mechanisms for peace, and how every achievement is so much less than it could and should have been. Woolcott, an energetic and personable man who has advanced through the ranks of the Australian foreign service since becoming a lawyer in 1977, inherited the file when the chance of an arms trade treaty seemed weak.

In the late 1990s, several non-governmental organizations, holding that the arms trade is a major cause of human rights abuses, began an advocacy campaign to regulate the booming business. The biggest importers are developing countries, some of whose governments spend more on military expenditure than on social development, communications infrastructure, and health combined. Since the US, Russia, Germany, France, and China are the principal sellers, opposing the military-industrial complexes in these powerful states is no easy matter. A group of Nobel Peace Prize laureates led by Óscar Arias, former president of Costa Rica, took up the cause. This introduced some diplomatic muscle and, in 2006, a group of states including Australia, Argentina, Costa Rica, Finland, Kenya, Japan, and the United Kingdom brought a resolution to the UN calling for work to begin on a treaty.

Only the United States, then under the administration of President George W. Bush, voted against. The proponents, taking their time, anticipated a new administration, and when Barack Obama arrived in the White House, the US engaged in the run-up to negotiations. A month-long conference under the leadership of Ambassador Roberto García Moritan of Argentina was set for July 2012. By that time, Obama was deep into his re-election campaign and the US wanted to keep the issue out of the election debates. The National Rifle Association, the obstreperous foe of arms control, appears to have intimidated US negotiators, who denied consensus even though the draft treaty was watered down several times to meet US demands. The US was not alone; Russia, China, and India also wanted lower standards, but maintained a lower profile. A band of seventy-four nations kept fighting for a stronger treaty, one without loopholes allowing arms to be diverted to unauthorized end-users. The only point of agreement was to try again in March 2013. Moritan went back to Argentina.

Ambassador Woolcott came on the scene determined to produce a text that would find the widest approval. "I did a huge amount of consultation in the months leading up to the final conference," he told me in the interview from his office in Geneva a few weeks after the negotiations. "I went to all the capitals of the permanent members of the Security Council, and also to India, to Cairo, to the Caribbean, to Mexico. There were more consultations in Geneva, Brussels, and New York. I was very careful not to unpick the threads of Moritan because I didn't want the whole July text to unravel. In the end, it was finally a judgment call, where the balance lay between competing interests, and giving everybody something and making everybody a little uncomfortable."

Many UN texts are produced by a process known as square brackets, i.e., what is not yet agreed to is put between square brackets and the delegates spend hours haggling over the contentious material. Woolcott bypassed this process and went straight to a single text. In the course of the conference, he revised the text twice and then, toward the end, announced delegates should "take it or leave it." This was a bold but risky strategy, since the US still insisted the treaty could be adopted only by consensus. In effect, although the US was now in favour of the treaty, Iran was handed a veto.

"In the end, you knew that the General Assembly would vote for the treaty, so how disappointed were you to be denied consensus?" I asked him.

"My mandate was to produce a strong, balanced and effective treaty," he said. "Obviously, I was aware that some states were working on Plan B, should consensus be denied. In the end, I think the final vote in the assembly was a good result, given the standing of the three countries [Iran, North Korea, and Syria] that were against it."

Whether a UN agreement is arrived at by consensus or a vote may seem academic, but effectiveness is at stake. The Arms Trade Treaty, a weak document because it was kept at the lowest common denominator in order to obtain consensus, was further weakened by a divisive vote. Nonetheless, it now exists. On the plus side, the treaty will help prevent the transfer of arms used to commit violations of human rights and international humanitarian law and stop unscrupulous arms dealers from operating with impunity. It establishes international standards that countries must incorporate into national control systems for the trade in conventional weapons. But it lacks comprehensive and binding prohibitions against the transfer of arms used in a wider array of human rights and international law violations. Its provisions covering ammunition, munitions, and components are weak. Compromise is its hallmark.

CIVIL SOCIETY ROLE "CRUCIAL"

Two leaders of Global Action to Prevent War — a small but effective non-governmental organization working to remove the institutional and ideological barriers that prevent the end of deadly conflict — attended all the convention sessions and are themselves divided over the efficacy of the treaty. I interviewed Bob Zuber and Katherine Prizeman over coffee at Nations Café, across the street from the UN.

"The treaty is historic; we've never had one before," Prizeman said. "It's consolidating a growing international norm that the transfer of arms should be regulated. In the beginning, some states scoffed at the idea of regulating the transfer of arms. After ten years of growing norm-building, we now have a sort of symbolic, somewhat practical piece of paper. That's a win. Whether it's actually going to change governments' decisions to transfer arms, the jury is still out."

Zuber, drawing on his long years of experience in peacemaking work, is critical of the process that produced the treaty and argues that states and non-governmental organizations should have put more time and energy into changing the culture of the arms trade before struggling to produce a piece of paper.

"I don't like the treaty, but is it worth having?" he asked and then answered his own question: "Yes." He doubts, however, that it will be effective.

Some NGOs, however, are far more bullish than Zuber. Bill Pace, executive director of World Federalist Movement and the Institute for Global Policy in New York, sees the treaty as a significant victory in the global movement to promote peace and security. "The treaty prohibits states from exporting conventional weapons in violation of arms embargoes, or weapons that would be used for acts of genocide, crimes against humanity, war crimes, or terrorism. This landmark agreement is the first treaty ever to recognize the link between gender-based violence and the international arms trade."

Ernie Regehr, founding executive director of Project Ploughshares (the premier disarmament group in Canada), cast a knowledgeable eye on the outcome. "Did we really think that states engaged in a lucrative industry worth billions of dollars and inextricably linked to their own self-perceived economic and security interest (as perverse as those perceptions might frequently be) would awake one morning to sign and seal a treaty that directly challenged all that?" he wrote on his blog. "That's not how states act. So the relevant question isn't whether the treaty is adequate to deal now with a destructive arms trade. It isn't. The relevant question is whether the treaty articulates basic principles of state responsibility and introduces the kinds of mechanisms and processes that can be employed over time to help shift perceptions of self-interest and to modify behaviour. And it does that."

Despite its weaknesses and ambivalences, the Arms Trade Treaty showed once again that pressure from civil society is the best way to galvanize political and diplomatic systems. This is the point made by Ken Epps, who in twenty-seven years with Project Ploughshares has followed the intricacies of the arms trade. I interviewed him by Skype after he returned to his office in Waterloo from monitoring the treaty negotiations.

The role of civil society, he said, "was crucial" throughout the years it took to achieve the treaty. "If it had not been for civil society, we would not have had an arms trade treaty, I'm entirely convinced of that. Non-governmental organizations not only originated the idea but campaigned for the treaty, bringing a one-million-names petition to the UN secretary-general. Once the process started, it was civil-society pressure that kept things on track. And partnership with key states finally gave us the treaty."

Epps says the treaty is a good one, considering it had to win the agreement of major actors in the arms trade. "For many of us who followed this from the beginning, it's better than we anticipated we would receive at the end of the process. There are some things that weren't achieved that we had hoped for, but one of the things won at the last moment was future-proofing of the treaty, where amendments will be allowed in future meetings and will be based on majority vote, not on consensus."

BUILDING GLOBAL NORMS

The incomplete victory that characterized the Arms Trade Treaty might well also describe the Anti-Personnel Mine Ban Convention of 1997 (the Landmines Treaty), which by now has proven its value in saving countless lives in many war-torn countries. The International Campaign to Ban Landmines, started by Jody Williams, who later won the Nobel Peace Prize for her leadership, also found resistance from major countries at first. The campaign used photos of young children killed and maimed by landmine explosions, often in areas where the children were playing, to turn a military subject into a humanitarian issue. The campaign created a global norm against landmines even if the treaty itself still lacks universal support.

The Landmines Treaty is a perfect example of what can be accomplished when vigorous civil society groups and like-minded governments work together. In this case, it was Canadian foreign minister Lloyd Axworthy who opened the diplomatic doors when he convened a meeting of like-minded governments to draft a treaty to ban landmines, an effort that became known as the "Ottawa Process."

In his memoir, *Navigating a New World*, Axworthy describes how moved he was by the destructive impact of landmines left over from wars or targeted at innocent civilians. In the mid-1990s, there were eighty-five to ninety million landmines planted in sixty countries. At the time, Human Rights Watch calculated between five and ten million landmines were produced each year. The estimated casualty rate was between thirty and forty thousand a year, with the most destruction in developing countries. It was not these statistics, horrifying as they were, that gripped public attention; rather, it was the first-hand stories of survivors often cradled in the arms of celebrities such as Princess Diana. Dramatic presentations of victims hit home with the public. Governments started to pay attention.

Axworthy laid the groundwork for a negotiating process that would bypass the normal UN disarmament forums that required the same consensus the Arms Trade Treaty failed to achieve. The only way to move beyond the "lowest common denominator" approach was to walk a different path, Axworthy wrote. "That walk began with citizens' groups. They were the ones who eventually yanked politicians and officials out of their comfortable chairs and forced them into stride." The negotiations to draft a treaty began among states that actually wanted a strong treaty, and when the draft was finished in a year's time, 120 states came to Ottawa for the formal adoption and signing. Within fifteen months, the requisite sixty ratifications were obtained and the treaty came into force on March 1, 1999.

I attended a ceremony in the Parliament Buildings in Ottawa marking the fifteenth anniversary of the adoption of the treaty. Axworthy, retired from politics and now president of the University of Winnipeg, was present, along with many of his officials of the day, including Jill Sinclair and Ralph Lysyshyn. Paul Hannon, director of Mines Action Canada, set a note not of jubilation but of the need to sustain political will to finish the job of removing all remaining landmines. His report was laden with statistics of success: for example, the destruction of forty-six million stockpiled mines in eighty-seven countries. More than 160 countries are now signatories to the treaty. What counts most is that human casualties are now less than a third of what they were before the treaty came into existence. "Landmines are stigmatized," Hannon told the gathering, "and most countries outside the treaty not only accept its goals but generally follow its obligations."

When we add the Convention on Cluster Munitions to the accomplishments of the Landmines Treaty and the Arms Trade Treaty, a pattern of at least some control over the arms industry emerges. In 2007, the government of Norway followed a similar process pioneered by Axworthy to build support for a ban on cluster munitions, weapons that eject clusters of submunitions ("bomblets") with delayed explosive force. Again, within a year the process produced a legally binding treaty, this one prohibiting the use and stockpiling of cluster munitions "that cause unacceptable harm to civilians." The signing ceremony in Dublin was attended by 107 nations, including seven of the fourteen countries that have used cluster bombs. By 2013, some seven hundred fifty thousand cluster munitions containing eighty-five million submunitions had been destroyed.

Similarly, the Chemical Weapons Convention, which came into effect in 1997, has resulted in more than 80 per cent of the declared chemical weapons stockpiles being destroyed.

Nonetheless, chemical weapons still exist and their use in the Syrian conflict provoked world outrage, leading to a UN Security Council resolution mandating inspectors to remove such weapons from Syria. The fifteen-year track record of the Organization for the Prohibition of Chemical Weapons, doing the often-dangerous work of disarmament, was recognized with the 2013 Nobel Peace Prize. The Biological Weapons Convention, dating back to 1972, was the first international agreement since the Second World War to provide for the elimination of a class of weapons. The continued enforcement of these bans is crucial to keeping weapons of mass destruction out of the hands of terrorists.

BETTER OFF THAN WE USED TO BE

Compared to preceding centuries, the world is in a more peaceful state, even though many people don't believe this. The professional organizations that study conflict and security issues, such as the Human Security Project of Simon Fraser University and the Stockholm International Peace Research Institute produce voluminous charts and statistics showing the decline in the number of wars since the two world wars as well as the Korean and Vietnam wars that engulfed the twentieth century. The last decade has seen fewer war deaths than in any other in the past century. The twenty-first-century wars in Afghanistan and Iraq and the protracted civil war in Syria are in the minds of the current generation, but they have not caused the big powers to fight one another. In fact, the old idea that war is necessary to stop aggression has been met with varying forms of disdain and resistance throughout the world. The rejection of war as a means of resolving conflict is growing, as President Obama found out when his threat to intervene militarily in Syria was rebuffed throughout the Western world.

Steven Pinker, a psychology professor at Harvard University, captured the big panorama of the decline in violent conflict in his book *The Better Angels of Our Nature: Why Violence Has Declined.* "The decline in violence may be the most significant and least appreciated development in the history of our species," he writes. "The developed nations did not fall into a third world war but rather a long peace." Even in the developing world, wars kill a fraction of the numbers they did a few decades ago. The world has moved on from the sadistic practices of the past, such as frivolous executions for public spectacle. Rape, battery, hate crimes, deadly riots, child abuse, cruelty to animals: The incidences of all of these are substantially down, and the public reacts vehemently against present-day instances; centuries ago, the public accepted such practices as the norm.

Many reviewers greeted Pinker's observations as a breath of fresh air, but a number of academics excoriated him for forgetting about continued "structural violence" against the poor, who suffer from the ceaseless excesses of the capitalist system in which the rich get richer at the expense of the poor, who do not share equitably in economic growth. He was accused of forgetting the warning of the Enlightenment thinker Thomas Hobbes, who held that the pursuit of power and glory drives humans into conflict. Recurrent violence, Pinker's critics said, is the result of the normal disorder of human life.

In November 2012, Pinker lectured to an overflow audience at Edmonton's Winspear Centre, and before he went on stage I interviewed him in the green room. He is a soft-spoken man, with the confidence of a trained academic but with a graceful demeanour. "You had a polarized reaction to your book, extreme praise and strong criticism. How do you assess this?" I asked him.

"It's shown me that it's very difficult to get people to think quantitatively. People think that if there's any violence remaining then the world is as bad as it ever was. To argue that we're not living in utopia, there's still violence but much less than there used to be, is a lesson that many people have trouble accepting. I think it's because many people are moralists, they want there to be some ongoing crisis that they can campaign against. The world always has to be getting worse in order to recruit more supporters."

Pinker added that the news media, which reports what happens, not what doesn't happen, is also partly responsible. "If there's some part of the world that hasn't had a war in the last twenty years, you never see a reporter there. Reporters are where the shells are exploding. Only when you look at the dogs that don't bark do you realize how much better off we are now than we used to be."

"Some people tell me that peace is impossible," I said.

"Yes, I've had a similar reaction," he responded. "People pay attention to what has happened, not what hasn't happened. If you ask people what's the situation in the world today, they talk about Syria or Somalia. Well, what about Angola, what about Mozambique, what about Nicaragua, what about Northern Ireland?"

Joshua S. Goldstein, a professor at American University and author of *Winning the War on War: The Decline of Armed Conflict Worldwide*, acknowledges that the US has been on a war footing since the terrorist attacks of September 11, 2001 and the consequent Afghanistan and Iraq wars proved to be longer, bloodier, and more expensive than anyone expected. But, he says, "Though the conflicts of the post-9/11 era may be longer than those of past generations, they're also far smaller and less lethal. America's decade of war since 2001 has killed about 6,000 U.S. service members compared with 58,000 in Vietnam and 300,000 in World War II." American troops are coming home from the latest wars and the American public has no appetite for more fighting. Goldstein adds: "President Obama was telling the truth when he said, 'The tide of war is receding.'"

FINDING OUR GLOBAL "MOJO"

A few months after the Landmines Treaty reunion in Ottawa, I talked to Lloyd Axworthy by phone about the progress in moving away from war — progress that is often hard to see because arms of one kind or another still inflict violence and havoc in many parts of the world. Axworthy has long been an advocate of "soft power," a concept that describes the ability to avoid or end a conflict through the tools of dialogue and mediation rather than the immediate use of military power. (In Chapter 4 I describe how Axworthy got the UN to accept the "Responsibility to Protect" doctrine.)

In the interview he drew my attention to the gains for human security now being made, however haltingly. The emphasis on arms reductions is the result of security being increasingly perceived in human not just national terms. "It's people who count," Axworthy said. "The Landmines Treaty also gave rise to the International Criminal Court, the Responsibility to Protect concept, and the whole idea of intervention to protect lives, and helped to create a framework for international humanitarian law, which is still in embryonic stage. Part of that precedent was the active co-operation between NGOs and a small group of governments. That didn't happen very often."

When Axworthy and I talked, the civil war in Syria was at its height, with the Security Council seemingly immobilized and, as Axworthy put it, "without any gumption to stop the killing." The council did later agree to send UN inspectors into Syria to remove all its chemical weapons, but it took this action only after public outrage on seeing photos of children who had suffered hideous deaths from chemical attacks. The large number of deaths in Syria resulting from conventional weapons had not stirred the council.

On his blog Axworthy had written, "It may just be that we are in a trough of poor leadership, divisive world politics, and an indifference to multilateral, cooperative solutions." I found that a trenchant comment, expressing exactly what I have been feeling for the last few years. Look around the world and try to find great political leaders with both vision and an ability to move the peace agenda forward. The paucity is depressing. I asked Axworthy to elaborate his view in the context of what the UN is trying to do to advance peacekeeping, peacebuilding, and the various mechanisms that are coming on stream.

"The deplorable Syrian situation demonstrates, if we ever needed further demonstration, that the present veto system has become anachronistic. This has become a huge hurdle to overcome. Second, this has become a generation where the idea of a consensus internationally of what needs to be done has become broken. There are no champions out there any more. Canada itself is no longer a champion for those kinds of principles. The Europeans are wound up in their financial woes. The Obama administration is forced by domestic politics and the two wars they fought to drop to a rear-sector kind of leadership. Russia will only be co-operative internationally when it is in its direct interests. China doesn't offer leadership. Maybe it's the 'me' generation. We have lost our global mojo to do anything that doesn't serve a particular national interest or advance the voodoo magic of the market."

He said political structures, including the UN itself, which is built around nation-state membership, are not designed to cope with modern, global issues, such as climate change and nuclear weapons. "We can't get our act together in any way, shape, or form on these huge problems."

Though he is politically battle-scarred, Axworthy is by no means despondent. "The world has experienced similar valleys of inaction and indifference before," he said. "We have proven ourselves capable to climb out of the darkest periods of human history to forge effective and united action. But it happens only if there continues to be a coterie of people around the world who believe that the values of peace and human security are important and can be activated."

A FEAR OF THE FUTURE

Axworthy's views, sharply etched, reflected the paradox of progress and impasse that characterize the modern world. It often appears as if the world is going in two different directions at the same time: gradually building instruments of peace and falling back to military tribalism. In the 1990s, the UN held a series of global conferences on the environment, food, water, housing, energy, women, and other key subjects. These meetings produced roadmaps showing the way forward. This momentum stalled after 9/11 and it has never recovered. Meetings in later years on human rights, climate change, and disarmament issues became fractious. A sense of fear, almost a fear of the future, pervaded international gatherings, especially as more terrorist acts followed 9/11.

In the new climate of fear, the gun industry thrives. With drones, the future of weaponry has arrived, and global strike weapons and "killer robots" are looming over the horizon. Cyberwarfare is already here and space weapons will be ready in a couple of generations. Machines are now replacing soldiers on the battlefield, and autonomous weapons, which can select targets without human intervention, are planned. The moral validity of such sophisticated weaponry — centering, of course, on the existing 17,000 nuclear weapons stationed in 111 sites in fourteen countries — needs to be fully examined, but moral questions are outmatched by the outreach of the military-industrial complex.

The gains made for humanity in the arms treaties I have described are important, but they pale beside the challenges ahead. In 2002, the Bush administration started targeting suspected Al-Qaeda leaders in Afghanistan, Yemen, and West

Pakistan with a new form of unmanned aerial vehicle called drones, remotely controlled from bases as far away as the US. President Obama picked up this new form of warfare and by 2013, the US had carried out some four hundred drone attacks in Yemen, Somalia, and Pakistan, killing between three thousand and forty-five hundred persons, including more than two hundred children, according to the Bureau of Investigative Journalism, a non-profit news organization in London. All this has been done in the name of the "global war on terror," which is not a precise armed conflict falling under the Geneva rules of warfare, but an amorphous response to the terrorist attacks of 9/11.

Many issues are opened by the arrival of drone warfare. Established international law is challenged when a powerful state can attack an enemy covertly, justifying its actions as the tactics of counterterrorism and counterinsurgency. The moral principles underlying the just war theory are flouted by the indiscriminate and disproportionate robot killing of many innocent civilians who happen to be near the strike zone. The US military wisdom of, in effect, challenging other governments to catch up to the latest technology, thereby setting a new arms race in motion, is reckless. Already, seventy countries possess some form of drone aircraft, most for surveillance and intelligence purposes, but increasingly for military use. The US has set a dangerous precedent with its aggressive and secretive drone attack programs. It is another act of political destabilization that makes it harder for the international community to find a common ground for security.

Former US President Jimmy Carter is outraged. Drone strikes and targeted assassinations "abet our enemies and alienate our friends," he wrote in the *Guardian* newspaper. America, he said, was "abandoning" its role as a champion of human rights. "Despite an arbitrary rule that any man killed by drones is declared an enemy terrorist, the death of nearby innocent women and children is accepted as inevitable . . . We don't know how many hundreds of innocent civilians have been killed in these attacks, each one approved by the highest authorities in Washington. This would have been unthinkable in previous times."

Much as I respect President Carter, with whom I have worked on nuclear disarmament issues, it is not historically correct to say that it was "unthinkable" for the US to kill innocent people in previous times. The US participated in the carpet-bombing of Dresden and other German targets in the Second World War, in which thousands of civilians were killed. And the atomic bombing of Hiroshima and Nagasaki directly killed more than two hundred thousand civilians. The defenders of drone attacks claim that selective targeting is a more ethical and effective way of conducting warfare. The White House claims they are "legal, ethical, and wise" and takes comfort in public opinion polls showing that Americans love drones because they are perceived as effective in reducing the threat of terrorism without endangering American lives. The US's defence of drones is not accepted by such countries as Brazil, China, and Venezuela, which used a UN debate on the subject to berate the US for abusing international law in its justification.

Drones illustrate the perplexity of trying to measure the effects of modern warfare. It can be argued that drones attack targets that in the past would have required an invasion with thousands of heavily armed troops, many of whom would have died along with displaced civilians. Overall violence is lessened. But the political astuteness is dubious. That is the state of the world today. The violence of warfare and the number of wars have diminished, certainly in quantitative terms, but the political machinery to build the conditions for peace lumbers, one might say staggers, along.

"WITHOUT HOPE, I'D BE DEAD"

Is the present trend line towards peace sustainable? To explore this further, I went to see my former colleague in the Canadian Senate, retired general Roméo Dallaire, a man whose terrible experiences as a UN commander in Rwanda in 1994 seared his mind. His book *Shake Hands With the Devil* describes the evil that shook him to the core. Dallaire now spends his life crusading against child soldiers and strengthening systems to prevent genocide. We sat in his Centre Block office on Parliament Hill, and he used a flip chart to describe the political, economic, and social improvements in Rwanda under President Paul Kagame. "Rwanda wants to become the Switzerland of Africa," he said. "The new infrastructure is incredible." Conditions in next-door Congo are still volatile, however, and that keeps the whole region unsettled.

"Can we use Rwanda as an example of a place where life was rebuilt and peace became possible despite the previous genocide, so humanity is not destined for continued wars?" I asked Dallaire.

"I believe that, although Darwinian concepts claim that we are continually in friction with one another for the best to survive," he answered. "Human beings have evolved to a higher level than survival and want to live in a serene environment where their hopes, aspirations, and potential can be maximized. With the advances in human rights and education and technology and the continued breaking down of geographical boundaries, maybe in a couple of centuries we can resolve our frictions without going to war."

This panoramic view of the progress of humanity from a man who has suffered enormously because of the suffering he witnessed has sustained him to stay alive and also given him a long-range perspective. "This is not short-term stuff, this is long-term stuff. When we went into Afghanistan, we should have had a fifty-year plan to rebuild the country. It's taken fifty years to settle down Cyprus and provide a stable environment. What's two hundred years to bring about a humanity resolving their frictions by other means than conflict after how many millennia of people slaughtering one another to try to achieve that? So I evolve trying to do my bit and hopefully influence enough people to keep humanity advancing so that maybe in two hundred years we can achieve the aim."

He said there are mornings when he wakes up thinking that the genocide he witnessed happened that morning rather than eighteen years ago. "It is that real. So eighteen years afterwards is peanuts in the time it takes to build peace."

"You're not dissuaded by the negative news of the day?" I asked him.

"No. Including the possibility of another civil war. There may be millions slaughtered and killed for centuries to come. But we are, through attrition, wearing down that old concept of continued conflict."

"Do you believe that violence is on a declining curve in historical terms?"

"Yes."

He said the world is at a transforming moment and is going through a series of revolutions. He listed "the environmental revolution where humanity and the planet have got to come to a communion because we want humanity not just to survive but thrive in the future." And also the communications revolution "where futurists are saying that within the next ten to fifteen years our method of deductive reasoning will not be able to handle the amount of information available." He said this would stimulate better political systems based on a new philosophical framework.

"The political tools of the past reached their zenith with the end of the Cold War. We have to adapt the old tools. National sovereignty is no more an absolute. Human sovereignty is now more important than national sovereignty. When human sovereignty is massively abused, we have a responsibility to go in and stop it. Already, the doctrine of the Responsibility to Protect has evolved. We've been at this for only twenty years."

The revolution that will sustain the concept of reduced conflict is that of the generation now under the age of twenty-five, he said. "I'm calling them the 'Generation Without Borders.' They function without any border. They are interconnected to the world. They can coalesce in real time with anybody in the world. And they're comfortable doing it. That generation will push aside those trapped in the old thinking that impedes conflict resolution."

"So you think we can be optimistic for peace because change is starting to happen?" I asked.

"If I didn't have this hope, I'd be dead."

CHAPTER 2:
A Global Ban on Nuclear Weapons

Wherever the abolition of nuclear weapons is discussed, the names Tadatoshi "Tad" Akiba and Hiroshima are practically synonymous. From 1999 to 2010, Akiba was the Mayor of Hiroshima and president of Mayors for Peace, an organization numbering 5,600 cities in 156 countries dedicated to eliminating the weapon that the president of the International Court of Justice called "the ultimate evil." The meaning of Hiroshima, where in 1945 140,000 people were killed in the first atomic attack, is too often lost among new generations oblivious to the continuing danger of nuclear weapons. Akiba's mission is to keep alive the memory of Hiroshima and Nagasaki, which suffered the same fate of massive atomic attack, so that a new generation of political leaders will finally do something to end the scourge of nuclear weapons. "Trying to predict the future is a tricky job," Akiba told me. "But people throughout the world want nuclear weapons gone. It's our job now to get the information about nuclear weapons out to the public in a massive outreach and mobilize the political will of leaders of the world."

This particular hour-long conversation took place by Skype, Akiba in Hiroshima and me in Edmonton, a fifteen-hour time change between us. But we have had personal meetings in many cities since we first met in his office in 1999. Akiba had just become Hiroshima's mayor, and one of his first projects was to revive Mayors for Peace, which was started in the 1980s but floundered for a while. Akiba brought in a new team and set a goal of 2020 for the complete elimination of nuclear weapons through the development of a global law. Vision and grit are his hallmarks.

Akiba's entanglements with the United States, a big obstacle to the fulfillment of his dream, are a fascinating leitmotif to his history. Tadatoshi Akiba was born November 3, 1942 in Tokyo. He remembers the bombing of his neighbourhood during the war. His family lived in poor conditions under the American occupation, especially after his father lost his job when the Japanese Imperial Army was disbanded. Akiba persevered in English studies and trained in judo, distinctions that earned him an exchange scholarship at Elmwood Park High School in a Chicago suburb. In Japan, the American authorities suppressed knowledge of the Hiroshima and Nagasaki bombings, so it was only at Elmwood that he began to learn the full story of the Second World War, including not only Hiroshima but also the Japanese attack on Pearl Harbor that drew the US into the war. He soon learned his American fellow students considered the atomic bomb "punishment" for Pearl Harbor.

Akiba returned to Japan for his university years and began specializing in mathematics. His skills as a simultaneous interpreter won him steady summer work at the annual World Conference Against Atomic and Hydrogen Bombs, which sprang up when a Japanese fishing boat, the *Lucky Dragon,* unknowingly entered the hydrogen bomb testing zone around Bikini Island and the crew was exposed to radiation fallout. Akiba made his first visit to Hiroshima in 1963 and started meeting the *hibakusha,* the Japanese term for survivors of the Hiroshima and Nagasaki attacks. Hearing their stories of appalling suffering changed his life. It was hard to find words to describe the terrible suffering. "They couldn't really express the terrible things that happened to them," Akiba recalled. "The one thing they all said was, 'This must never happen again to anyone.' Their essential message was reconciliation, not retaliation." That theme has permeated the rest of Akiba's life.

HUMANITARIAN, NOT IDEOLOGICAL

In 1968, Akiba returned to the US and earned his Ph.D. in topology from the Massachusetts Institute of Technology. This led to a teaching offer at State University of New York. He married and soon switched to teaching mathematics at Tufts University, Boston. When his son James was growing up, Akiba worried that the boy needed a deeper understanding of what happened at Hiroshima. The prevailing attitude around Tufts, he said, was that the American atomic bombing had been justified. He started a project to bring American journalists to Hiroshima for first-hand research. It became so popular it was named the "Akiba Project." He returned home for a sabbatical in 1986. This was another turning point: Akiba decided to stay in Japan; his wife returned to the US. Akiba, the *hibakusha* advocate, was now a celebrity in Hiroshima and, in 1990, was elected under the banner of the Japan Socialist Party to a seat in the House of Representatives.

Under the conservative Liberal Democratic Party, which hewed closely to US foreign policy, Japan stayed closely under the US nuclear deterrence umbrella. The very country that had suffered the effects of the early nuclear weapons was limp in its protestations against them. Akiba found the Socialist Party ineffective in its opposition. When the Hiroshima mayoralty opened up, Akiba ran. "I thought I could do just as good a job as mayor to promote peace and make Japanese democracy work better."

"We created a roadmap for Mayors for Peace to reach out

around the world. Then 9/11 happened and the *hibakusha* became really concerned because the new war against terrorism opened up the possibility that the Bush administration might somehow use nuclear weapons. We quickly developed a '20/20 Vision' program, which aimed at the elimination of nuclear weapons by 2020." Mayors for Peace runs cultural and academic programs, collects signatures on petitions, and sends delegations to important nuclear disarmament diplomatic meetings.

"Mayors for Peace became an important organization around the world, especially as you went over the 5,000 cities mark," I said. "How do you assess its impact?"

"Nuclear weapons issues in those years had been seen ideologically, and many people stayed away from the movement because they did not want to get into an ideological battle," he said. "During the US-Soviet Cold War, people felt they had to be on one side or the other of the ideological struggle. Getting into the nuclear disarmament movement meant that you were characterized on 'the left.' Many people rejected this labelling because they felt a humanitarian, not a political motivation. When Mayors for Peace stood up without any ideology, people started to see nuclear disarmament as something they could identify with. The movement grew because we were not ideological, rather humanitarian." After three terms, Akiba stepped down from the mayoralty and accepted the chairmanship of the Middle Powers Initiative, a consortium of eight civil society organizations specializing in nuclear disarmament issues, which holds consultations among like-minded governments.

A TWO-CLASS NUCLEAR WORLD

The centrepiece of these discussions is how to strengthen the Non-Proliferation Treaty (NPT), an agreement embracing 190 states dating back to 1970 under which states without nuclear weapons agreed to not acquire nuclear weapons in return for the acknowledged nuclear weapon states (the US, Russia, China, United Kingdom, and France) entering into good faith negotiations to eliminate their nuclear arsenals. The NPT also permits states to develop nuclear energy for peaceful purposes, an issue at the heart of the Iranian problem. Iran claims its enrichment of uranium is for peaceful use, but Western states for years held that Iran was using this as a pretext for converting nuclear technology for a bomb.

While the international spotlight has been on Iran's nuclear program and North Korea's testing of nuclear weapons, the heart of the nuclear weapons problem remains the intransigence of the five permanent members of the Security Council, the same five original members of the nuclear weapons club. From the moment of the Trinity flash in the skies of New Mexico, the United States, Russia (then the Soviet Union), the United Kingdom, France, and then China engaged in the development of their nuclear arsenals. At the peak of the Cold War, in the early 1980s, some 65,000 nuclear weapons existed, about 95 per cent of them in the hands of the two superpowers of the day. Now the arsenals have diminished, with about seventeen thousand still in existence. India, Pakistan, Israel, and North Korea have joined the nuclear weapons club and the major states are determined that Iran will not.

Even though calls for nuclear disarmament escalated through the years, the nuclear weapons states have consistently dodged any real efforts for nuclear disarmament. Those who negotiated the NPT in the late 1960s gave themselves a massive loophole in the famous Article VI, which enjoins states to enter into good faith negotiations for nuclear disarmament by joining this obligation to a similar one for general and complete disarmament. To wait for the world to become a perfectly peaceful place before abolishing nuclear weapons completely misses the point that it is the maintenance of nuclear weapons that destabilizes world conditions. A two-class world in which the powerful aggrandize unto themselves nuclear weapons while proscribing their acquisition by other states is not sustainable. We face the danger of nuclear weapon proliferation because the powerful nuclear states have not used their authority to build a specific law outlawing all nuclear weapons. The International Court of Justice in 1996 ruled that nuclear disarmament is a singular obligation, and unanimously stated that all states have a duty to negotiate the elimination of nuclear weapons.

The US and Russia have engaged in bilateral rounds of reductions, but the trumpeting of lower numbers has masked their continued modernization of warheads, delivery systems, and infrastructure. The 2013 Yearbook of the Stockholm International Peace Research Institute states that the nuclear weapons powers, which continue to deploy new nuclear weapons and delivery systems, "appear determined to retain their nuclear arsenals indefinitely." There are, thankfully, fewer nuclear weapons now, but their explosive power (some two thousand strategic weapons are kept on constant alert) is still horrendous.

A double standard has deeply conflicted NATO, which continues to claim that the possession of nuclear weapons provides the "supreme guarantee" of the security of its twenty-six member states. At one and the same time, the NATO states reaffirm their commitment to the NPT goal of nuclear disarmament while maintaining NATO's dependence on nuclear weapons. The policies are incoherent. The US, the UK, and France, the three Western nuclear powers sometimes known as the "P3," drive NATO and have made it the world's biggest nuclear-armed alliance. The continued deployment of US tactical nuclear bombs on the soil of Belgium, Germany, the Netherlands, Italy, and Turkey, though resisted by growing numbers of people in those countries, is a standing provocation to Russia, which is consequently disinclined to lower its own huge numbers of tactical nuclear weapons. Russia is unlikely to give up its nuclear weapons while it is virtually surrounded by an expanding NATO.

Despite cuts to superfluous systems, nuclear arsenals have become normalized as an integral part of security systems. In the next decade, nuclear weapons possessors will spend $1 trillion modernizing these nuclear systems. They are clearly planning for a future with nuclear weapons rather than their elimination. The UK, France, and China say they will not engage in multilateral negotiations for nuclear disarmament until the two major powers have reduced their stocks to much lower levels than at present. But US-Russia bilateral negotiations for deeper cuts are stalled over such issues as the US's proposed missile defence system in Europe, the militarization of space, and the US's intention to militarily dominate air, land, sea, space, and cyberwarfare. Nuclear disarmament is inevitably caught up in geopolitical tensions.

BAN KI-MOON'S PLAN

The nuclear weapons possessors say that as long as nuclear weapons exist, they will have to keep theirs. The voracious military-industrial complex, making ever-increasing amounts of money through the modernization programs, feeds this insidious thinking. "Extended" deterrence, by which the US guarantees to protect its allies from attack, is now a permanent policy. However, many who once championed nuclear deterrence are having second thoughts. Four American statesmen — Henry Kissinger, George Schultz, William Perry, and Sam Nunn — who have been writing in the *Wall Street Journal* on this subject, said: "The risk that deterrence will fail and that nuclear weapons will be used increases dramatically." They added: "Global leaders owe it to their publics to reduce, and eventually to eliminate, these risks."

In 2008, UN Secretary-General Ban Ki-moon suggested that the international community start work on a Nuclear Weapons

Convention. This would be a treaty banning the production as well as deployment of nuclear weapons. A group of civil society leaders had produced a model convention in the late 1990s and it subsequently became a UN document. Ban Ki-moon's support led to a series of resolutions in the UN's Disarmament Committee, which showed widespread support for the idea. More than three-quarters of the countries of the world have voted to commence negotiations leading to the conclusion of a Nuclear Weapons Convention. Support comes from across the geo-political spectrum, including from Asia, Africa, the Middle East, Latin America, and parts of Europe, and includes support from some of the countries possessing nuclear weapons, including China, India, Pakistan, and North Korea. Nations supporting a ban make up 81 per cent of the world's population. More support is coming from such important groups as the Inter-Action Council — twenty former heads of state from key countries, including the US, Canada, Norway, Germany, Japan, and Mexico — and the December 2011 Summit of Leaders of Latin American and Caribbean States. The NATO bloc and Russia remain sternly opposed.

Akiba is determined to overcome the stalemate over comprehensive negotiations and reach as many politicians, diplomats, and journalists as possible with a message of conscience joined to this practical program for the elimination of nuclear weapons. He wants like-minded governments to start preparatory work for a convention. "Our aim is the verified, irreversible, transparent, legally binding, and universal reduction and elimination of nuclear arsenals within the foreseeable future, on a definite schedule," he told me. "A comprehensive approach would reinforce and stimulate partial measures such as the test ban treaty and further US-Russian reductions on the existing agenda."

A BREACH OF FAITH

The major states' opposition to comprehensive negotiations has become so blatant that Judge Christopher Weeramantry, former vice-president of the International Court of Justice (the highest legal authority in the world), has charged them with breach of faith. Article VI of the NPT stipulates that each of the parties to the treaty "undertakes to pursue negotiations *in good faith* on effective measures relating to cessation of the nuclear arms race at an early date . . ." (emphasis added). Weeramantry contends that continued research on nuclear weapons, increasing their range and effectiveness and deploying them by land, sea, and air "are in positive violation of the solemn duty of good faith lying upon the nations committing these acts." Furthermore, he writes, their actions are prompting other states to join the "nuclear club."

I have known Weeramantry for many years and interviewed him by Skype at his home in Sri Lanka where he started the Weeramantry International Center for Peace Education and Research after retiring from the International Court of Justice. "Does the negotiation of the elimination of nuclear weapons have to await the development of more international law?" I asked

"Not at all," he said. "International law is already replete with principles that prohibit weapons of this sort. In 1899, the nations of the world agreed that the expanding bullet, known as the dumdum bullet, was too cruel to be used in warfare among civilized nations. The same system of law cannot tolerate nuclear weapons, which create suffering a million times greater. Suffering imposed by nuclear weapons extends not only to people now living but goes down to future generations. What right have we to damage the environment and injure future generations? I think that's an absolutely barbarous thing to do."

"But the nuclear weapons states are ignoring humanitarian law," I said, "and rendering it ineffective. How can we influence them to inject 'good faith' into their actions?"

"We must draw attention to this at every level," he said. "For a long time, I have been advocating that peace education be made compulsory in all schools, because children are now growing up as future world citizens not knowing a shred of information about international law. Students must be made aware of the principles of international law. This is not just for experts. Every citizen needs to know something of it. Good faith is ingrained in international law and is one of its strengths. Good faith means that if you give an assurance or an undertaking you have to do it in good faith. You can't have one principle in mind and then pretend to do something else. In the case of nuclear weapons, you have a unanimous decision of the highest international court in the world saying that an obligation lies on every nuclear power in good faith to take steps to reduce their nuclear arsenals. This must be brought home to those in the corridors of power, who often shut their eyes to basic obligations. These obligations must be known and respected. The general public must understand this so they can put pressure on their rulers to obey international law."

A FRESH PERSPECTIVE

After a while, nuclear disarmament can seem to be just a revolving circle of meetings and speeches. Needing a fresh perspective, I sought out two young women whose work with Reaching Critical Will had impressed me. Reaching Critical Will is the disarmament program of the Women's International League for Peace and Freedom, the oldest women's peace organization in the world. It was founded in April 1915 in The Hague by some thirteen hundred women from Europe and North America (including neutral countries and those at war with each other) who came together to protest the killing and destruction of the war then raging in Europe. Reaching Critical Will does critical analyses of current issues and publishes daily reports when important disarmament meetings are taking place, which even delegates rely on to tell them what's going on. These reports, distributed electronically to a wide list of followers around the world, are produced by Ray Acheson, operating out of Reaching Critical Will's New York office, and by Beatrice Fihn in the Geneva office.

I met Ray for coffee one morning in New York as she was putting the final touches on an updated version of *Assuring Destruction Forever: Nuclear Weapon Modernization Around the World*, a book she edited in 2012. The book is an in-depth professional examination of how all the nuclear weapons states are modernizing their arsenals. "At the same time as they commit billions of dollars to their nuclear weapon arsenals, most of these states are simultaneously making significant cuts in their social welfare systems, such as health care, education and childcare," she wrote in the introduction. A Canadian, Acheson did a Bachelor of Arts in peace and conflict studies at the University of Toronto and was pursuing a Master's degree at the New School in social research.

I asked her why she concentrated on nuclear disarmament when most people hardly think of the subject.

"I think nuclear weapons are an excellent example of skewed priorities in the world, and the hypocrisy of international relations," she said. "They're a perfect metaphor for everything that's wrong in the world. I know a lot of people think you're some sort of utopian idealist if you think nuclear disarmament is possible. Even some people who've worked on these issues their whole lives think there's nothing can be done. There are some days when the whole thing seems completely intractable. On the other hand, there are a lot of things happening recently that have given me renewed energy."

She pointed to states such as Austria, Norway, and Mexico, starting to say, "Enough is enough," and Norway hosting 127 states to discuss the catastrophic humanitarian consequences of nuclear weapons. Even though the major nuclear powers boycotted the meeting, their obstinacy held them up to ridicule. "Right before the governmental meeting in Oslo, we had a civil society forum attended by 450 people from seventy countries. At least half of those people were under thirty. I've never seen such strong youth representation before."

"That's a good sign," I said, "but do you think I'm wrong in what I found on a speaking tour of universities, that most young people, while caring of the human condition, don't have any understanding of nuclear disarmament and thus future generations will be even less knowledgeable?"

"For the most part, I think you're right," she responded. "I used to have the same impression. Nuclear weapons were never discussed, even in my university program of peace and conflict studies. Young people who are committed to social justice are much more focused on climate change or the Occupy movement. But the International Campaign to Abolish Nuclear Weapons is making a strong appeal to youth. So maybe that's contributing to more youth awareness."

"What about young women getting into this field?" I asked her. "As women continue to take important positions in the political and societal processes, do you see more women moving into decision-making processes in nuclear disarmament?"

"That's a good question," she said, then paused before continuing. "I think yes."

"Let me put the question more sharply," I said. "I'm an old white guy, and I truly believe that if more women were in decision-making processes in nuclear disarmament, we'd have a more humane world. Can I hope that the younger generation will do a better job on this than we did, and within that new generation, there will be more women?"

"I think you can," she said. "Attitudes towards women's participation will continue to evolve. There's a lot pushback against that, mostly from 'old white men,' but a new generation of men is moving forward. Nuclear disarmament is too often seen as a niche field full of technical jargon, and women's participation in this has to be connected to their overall capacity. We have to get beyond the limitation of the old gender roles."

A CONSTANT REMINDER OF IMMENSE SUFFERING

The professional level of Ray Acheson's work and that of her colleague, Beatrice Fihn, would challenge many of the diplomats who walk the halls of the UN. Fihn has just edited a new publication, *Unspeakable Suffering: The Humanitarian Impact of Nuclear Weapons,* which is a devastating analysis that society does not have the infrastructure to cope with a nuclear attack. She described her work: "By focusing on the humanitarian impact and consequences of nuclear weapons, it becomes clear that these weapons are simply inhumane, unacceptable, and appalling weapons of terror. Just like chemical and biological weapons, no state should be proud to possess them or aspire to acquire them. Maintaining nuclear weapons is not a symbol of power or strength, but instead a constant reminder of the immense suffering that they have caused and continuously threaten to cause again."

I wanted to know how she got into this field, so I interviewed her by Skype in her home in Geneva. She and her husband had just put their two-year-old daughter to bed and Beatrice was ready for her daily run. After graduating from Stockholm University in her native Sweden, Fihn earned a Master's degree in law at London University and joined the Women's International League for Peace and Freedom in Geneva as an intern. "Ray and I got to know each other as interns and started a trans-Atlantic collaboration doing complementary work for Reaching Critical Will. We keep in constant contact through email and Skype."

I asked her what effect her new book was having in the diplomatic debates, given that the powerful states never like to talk about the humanitarian consequences of their nuclear policies and even boycotted the Norway-sponsored meeting on the subject. "The new emphasis on catastrophic humanitarian consequences of nuclear warfare seems to be making the nuclear weapons states a bit nervous," she said. "The consequences are not a new idea, but the humanitarian approach reclaims the debate and puts the focus on getting rid of the nuclear weapons. That's the only guarantee they will never be used. We're hearing this approach from more and more countries."

Seventy-eight countries have signed a statement emphasizing the incalculable human suffering associated with any use of nuclear weapons, and the implications for international humanitarian law. Fihn sees a new dynamic entering the diplomatic discussions. "There's a new energy and courage in many states — not the NATO states, of course, they're terrified of this. But we're proving we can advance the discussion without the participation of the nuclear weapons states."

I congratulated her for maintaining her running schedule amid so many commitments at home and work. "It's a moment of peace," she said.

PRESIDENTS AND PRIME MINISTERS GALORE

I have attended seven of the review conferences of the Non-Proliferation Treaty, which are held every five years, and as Canadian Ambassador for Disarmament at the time, I led the Canadian delegation at the 1985 review conference. Most reviews have ended in discord, but the 1985 meeting actually produced a final consensus document. The only catch was that in its opening lines the document said the conference had agreed that delegates could not agree on the main points. At the 2000 review, the delegates did come to an agreement on a thirteen-step action plan, the heart of which the United States, with George W. Bush coming into power the following year, promptly revoked. Mostly, the meetings through the years have amounted to a ritualistic façade. By their actions at these conferences and related meetings, the nuclear weapons states have given a new meaning to hypocrisy.

Many times I have to resist becoming jaded at the prospect of attending yet another such gathering. Yet I was intrigued when, for the first time in the history of the UN, the General Assembly called a high-level meeting on nuclear disarmament on September 26, 2013. I went to New York for the meeting and sat through an extravaganza of seventy-four speeches over an eight-and-a-half-hour period. From nearly every corner of the world — Europe, Africa, Asia, Latin America — a plethora of presidents, prime ministers, and other high officials called for active work to start comprehensive negotiations to lead to a world free of nuclear weapons.

UN Secretary-General Ban Ki-moon, who recalled that five years ago he had launched his Five-Point Plan for Nuclear Disarmament and Non-Proliferation, said, "I was profoundly moved to be the first United Nations Secretary-General to attend the Peace Memorial Ceremony in Hiroshima. I also visited Nagasaki. Sadly, we know the terrible humanitarian consequences from the use of even one weapon. As long as such weapons exist, so, too, will the risks of use and proliferation." Several speakers quoted the Secretary-General's earlier words, "There are no right hands for the wrong weapons." Ban Ki-moon was followed by President Heinz Fischer of Austria, who said, "Nuclear weapons should be stigmatized, banned, and eliminated before they abolish us."

Many speakers gave impassioned warnings of the "catastrophic humanitarian consequences" of nuclear weapons, some gave perfunctory and somewhat ritualistic calls for progress in nuclear disarmament, and a tiny minority criticized the holding of the special meeting. An unknown mid-level British official took the floor on behalf of the US, UK, and France to deliver a rebuke to the General Assembly for even holding such a meeting.

She said the three Western nuclear powers "regretted" the extraordinary meeting and she chastised the delegates to get back to the "step-by-step" approach to nuclear disarmament, to which the Philippine delegate responded, "The step-by-step approach has become synonymous to foot dragging."

Usually, the five major nuclear powers present a united front at nuclear disarmament meetings. The high-level meeting revealed that they are no longer united, for China's Director-General of Arms Control, Pang Sen, welcomed the special meeting and called on the international community to develop "a convention on the complete prohibition of nuclear weapons." Russia's Deputy Director of Security Affairs and Disarmament, Alexey Karpov, said his country would move ahead if "pragmatic principles" were met. As a first step, Russia wants NATO's tactical nuclear weapons removed from Europe. Russia is unwilling to negotiate with the US on further reductions of strategic weapons until it feels the issues of the US missile defence system in Europe, space weapons, and conventional force imbalances are satisfactorily addressed. It also wants the Comprehensive Test Ban Treaty brought into force, an event that will not happen until the US ratifies it. "Without such conditions," Karpov said, "it is hard to imagine that nuclear disarmament would have any prospects." Clearly, Russia wants to negotiate with the United States on a partnership basis, but the US, still wedded to its claim of "exceptionalism," insists on maintaining a superior military status. That is the heart of the nuclear disarmament problem.

The star of the high-level meeting was undoubtedly Iran's new president, Hassan Rouhani, who came to the podium on behalf of the 120 non-aligned nations to condemn any use of nuclear weapons as "a crime against humanity" and propose early commencement of negotiations in the Conference on Disarmament to prohibit the possession, development, and use of nuclear weapons. Iran's new stance under Rouhani has subsequently led to the development of better relations with the US, but there is still a long distance to go to get Obama's bureaucracy to implement the nuclear disarmament goals set out by their president.

After the meeting ended, I sought out Jayantha Dhanapala, a Sri Lankan diplomat who is one of the leading figures in the world on nuclear disarmament. He deftly presided over the 1995 Review Conference of the Non-Proliferation Treaty, which made the treaty permanent, and later became the UN Under-Secretary-General for Disarmament Affairs. He was a candidate for Secretary-General in 2006. I first met Dhanapala in 1984 when we were both our respective countries' disarmament ambassadors and recognized at first glance that we were kindred souls.

"Does the fact that the high-level meeting was held mean that governments will give more political attention to the issue?" I asked him.

"It was a high-level meeting with low expectations," he said. "The possessor countries will do very little to get rid of their nuclear weapons. There is no movement in US-Russian bilateral negotiations, despite the pious rhetoric of Mr. Obama. He has been a big disappointment to the disarmament community. He encouraged us to think ambitiously about a nuclear weapons–free world, but he has not taken practical steps to achieve that." It was an irony, he said, that the prospects for a political peace in some of the trouble spots in the world are improving while the prospects for nuclear disarmament remain dim. "We need to continue our pressure in civil society for a Nuclear Weapons Convention because it is only a convention that will eliminate nuclear weapons."

Dhanapala castigated what he called "the hypocrisy" of those who denounced chemical weapons while blithely holding onto nuclear weapons, which are much more lethal than chemical weapons. "Do we have to wait for a ghastly nuclear accident or nuclear terrorism for people to come to their senses?"

PASSIVE PUBLIC OPINION

While the nuclear weapons states bear the major responsibility for the nuclear weapons dilemma, other factors also play a role. The non-nuclear states are timid in pressing the case for abolition. The mainstream media mostly ignores the issue. Informed societal leadership, particularly in the academic, religious, and scientific communities, is absent. Public opinion, particularly since the end of the Cold War, has become amorphous. The world seems not to have heard the admonition of the 2010 NPT Review conference: "All states need to make special efforts to establish the necessary framework to achieve and maintain a world without nuclear weapons." Ridding the world of the ultimate evil must be a joint effort.

Nuclear abolitionists are fond of saying, "The public is on our side." Indeed, important polls have generally shown that a heavy majority of the public supports the idea of a legal ban on nuclear weapons. When asked the question directly, most people favour the elimination of nuclear weapons. That, of course, is a better situation than we would find ourselves in if most people wanted the retention of nuclear weapons. But, for the most part, public opinion is so passive as to rarely register on any list of public concerns. With the end of the Cold War, nuclear weapons went out of people's minds. A bright university student told me, "I don't even think about the fact that I don't think about nuclear weapons." A nuclear abolitionist who turned thirty said his friends at the birthday party all expressed amazement that he would spend so much time on an issue they deemed passé.

With the public mostly oblivious to the issue, there is little if any pressure put on governments to take concrete steps to end the danger. The issue is almost never mentioned in election campaigns, and the average elected politician, those we normally consider informed on current events, has a kindergarten-level understanding of the role that nuclear weapons play in preventing the development of the conditions for peace. Those parliamentarians and even many civil society advocates who do get into nuclear weapons issues often succumb to what is considered the higher level of knowledge of the officials and technocrats who treat the subject as a numbers game instead of an expression of our deepest morality as human beings. The public is still intimidated by the "experts."

Disarmament education, started valiantly by the UN in the 1980s, has fallen by the wayside. Defence studies now grab the lion's share of public funds. We are turning out university students who regard nuclear weapons as just part of the "furniture" of life. There is a little nuclear abolition activity on the campuses, thanks to the Global Zero movement, but the paucity of student activism pales compared with the campus advocacy of the 1980s.

It is ironic that the steam has gone out of the nuclear disarmament movement at the very moment that President Obama has won the Nobel Peace Prize for pointing to the possibility of a nuclear weapons–free world. The awarding of the prize should have been followed by mass rallies around the world supporting this goal. But a general indifference set in. With little political support, Obama lowered his expectations. The modernization of nuclear weapons continues.

There is a striking contrast between the ardent activism of civil society groups campaigning for nuclear disarmament and the apathy of the general public. Civil society activists have in the past created public pressure that kept governments from the nuclear brink and they deserve much credit. The American historian Lawrence Wittner, who has written extensively on peace movements, says public opinion is responsible for the gains that have been made in lowering the numbers of nuclear weapons. "Governments can be convinced to adopt policies of nuclear restraint," he said in a lecture I attended in Ottawa, "if there is sufficient public pressure. When that pressure has been mobilized by disarmament activists, governments have responded — curbing the nuclear arms race and rejecting nuclear war. If the full strength of public sentiment can be brought to bear on government officials, humanity might just manage to take one very important step further: establish a nuclear-free world and end the threat of nuclear annihilation forever."

Civil society movements contain highly knowledgeable and courageous individuals, and we should be grateful for this. A new coalition, the International Campaign to Abolish Nuclear Weapons (ICAN), has gathered some three hundred organizations in seventy countries to mobilize people to work for a Nuclear Weapons Convention. One of its spokespersons, Nosizwe Lise Baqwa, a young Norwegian mother of South African parentage, spoke at the UN high-level meeting on nuclear disarmament, telling the delegates, "That nuclear weapons have not already been clearly declared illegal for all . . . is a failure of our collective social responsibility."

The sense of social responsibility is growing. Humanitarian, environmental, human rights, peace, and development organizations are joining together to present a common front to the nuclear powers. The ICAN coalition has made a promising start, reflecting the determination of core groups throughout the world to free humanity from the spectre of its own destruction. When they reach critical mass, they may yet move the levers of power.

CHAPTER 3:
The Development Agenda Expands

Helen Clark greeted me graciously when I entered her spacious office on the twenty-first floor of One United Nations Plaza, directly across First Avenue from the UN Building in New York. I first met her at the UN in the 1980s when she was a new Member of Parliament before becoming the Rt. Hon. Helen Clark, Prime Minister of New Zealand. Now she is the highly respected and politically astute Administrator of the United Nations Development Programme (UNDP), which runs anti-poverty, crisis prevention, democratic governance, and environmental projects around the world. There was a smile on her face this morning as she looked over advance proofs of the *2013 Human Development Report*. It was full of good news about major development gains in Africa, Asia, and Latin America.

The rise of the South, to use a more specific term encompassing the lands that used to be called developing countries, is unprecedented in its speed and scale. "A new global middle class is emerging, with hundreds of millions of people lifted out of poverty," she told me. "Never in history have living conditions and prospects of so many people changed so dramatically and so fast."

Helen Clark was first elected as a Labour member in the New Zealand House of Representatives in 1981, played a major role in the country's adoption of an anti-nuclear policy, which strained relations with the US, then slogged her way through a variety of ministerial posts before becoming Prime Minister in 1999. Under her premiership, New Zealand strongly opposed the Iraq War but contributed to the US-led campaign against the Taliban and Al-Qaeda in Afghanistan and later helped in post-war reconstruction in Iraq. During the Iraq war, Clark publicly suggested that the conflict would not have happened had former Vice-President Al Gore won the 2000 election, so it was fortunate that a like-minded President Obama had arrived on the scene by the time Clark, defeated after three terms as Prime Minister, was nominated in 2009 for the number-three post in the UN hierarchy. She was elected unanimously by the UN General Assembly as the first woman to head the UNDP, and *Forbes* magazine named her one of the most powerful women in the world.

Clark sat across from me at a coffee table as we began to talk about how the concept and practices of human development have changed drastically over the years from aid presented as charity to a complex array of programs to help people fend off the ravages of war. I pointed out that when I started writing about development in the 1970s, the standard figure for the number of people living in dire poverty was about one billion. That's still more or less the figure today (UN Secretary-General Ban Ki-moon says almost one billion people will still be living on less than $1.25 a day by 2015). Since 1970, however, the world population has doubled, so the real gains in reducing poverty across the world are tremendous. And those gains are coming at a faster rate as a result of sustained investment in education, health care, and social programs.

Clark is by no means alone in her jubilation at what has happened. As Kishore Mahbubani, Dean of the Lee Kuan Yew School of Public Policy at the National University of Singapore and former Ambassador to the UN, says in his 2013 book, *The Great Convergence,* "Never before in human history have so many people been lifted out of absolute poverty. Simple things like a flush toilet, electricity at home, a cell phone, a TV set, and a refrigerator have represented the aspirations of billions. For a long time, they seemed out of reach. Today, 500 million Asians enjoy middle class standards. By 2020, this number will explode to 1.75 billion, an increase of three-and-a-half times in eight years."

"The decline of war has been a big factor in this spurt of development," Clark said. "UNDP is now better able to focus on human rights, democracy, and good governance as intrinsic to good government and human security for all." She showed me the early documents for a project dear to her heart, the Post-2015 UN Development Agenda. The first words of the first report on this subject convey the scale of the endeavour: "The central challenge of the post-2015 UN development agenda is to ensure that globalization becomes a positive force for all the world's peoples of present and future generations."

As I listened to her describe the project and later talked to some of her colleagues, I began to see how reduced warfare and military expenditure, more sophisticated development processes, and higher standards for protecting the planet are all strengthening the foundation for greater security in the world. It takes a political mind to steer through the shoals of greed and stupidity that still afflict much of the political system. With her charm and steel, Helen Clark seems to be managing. She is driving her colleagues forward.

DEVELOPING HUMAN SECURITY

We have to step back for a moment and see what she is building on. How did development transmogrify from simple aid projects (the digging of a well for clean water is still a life-saving need) to complex institutions of government?

In 1971, A UN commission headed by Canada's Lester B. Pearson established an Official Development Assistance target of 0.7 per cent of the gross national product of the developed countries to be devoted to aiding developing countries. While the interplay of structural questions of trade, investment, and finance were also discussed, the public generally saw the relationship between the developed and developing as one of the transfer of a small amount of resources to the poor. And economic development of both rich and poor was usually measured by the gross domestic product of each country. If a country's overall economic statistics were on the upswing, it was considered to be advancing. This statistics approach cloaked the continuing poverty of the most vulnerable, as I found out for myself in a series of trips I made to developing countries in the 1970s and 1980s.

One day in 1979, I walked through the outskirts of Yaounde, the capital of Cameroon in Central Africa. I came upon a wailing party, and met the father of a two-year-old boy who had just been buried. The man invited me into his house to meet his wife and children. "How did your little boy die?" I asked. He pointed to his stomach. "Dysentery?" I asked. Yes, he said.

"Where do you get your water?" I asked.

The man led me down the street to a dirty mud creek where children were playing and women were washing clothes.

"You drink that water!" I exclaimed.

"Well," he said, "actually up on the hill, there's a pipe with clean water. But you have to pay and it only works four hours a day. The kids don't have any money so they drink out of the creek." When the man told me the story of his child, he spoke for the millions of parents who lose their children every year because of water-borne diseases.

As the 1980s progressed, new ideas entered the development debate. The effect of militarism had been raised earlier by US President Dwight D. Eisenhower, who said, "Every gun that is made, every warship launched, every rocket fired, signifies, in a final sense, a theft from those who hunger and are not fed, from those who are cold and are not clothed." A three-year study of the relationship between disarmament and development, headed by the formidable Swedish diplomat Inga Thorsson, reported in 1981: "The world has a choice. It can continue to pursue the arms race or it can move with deliberate speed towards a more sustainable economic and political order. It cannot do both. . . . A compelling appeal can be made to the economic self-interest of states to reduce military expenditure and reallocate resources to development." Thorsson's case essentially was that security was strengthened by moving down the two paths of disarmament and development at the same time.

By 1987, the UN was ready to hold a conference on the subject. The US refused to attend on the grounds it did not believe there was any relationship between disarmament and development. Other Western nations were cool to the idea because they perceived the meeting as an attempt by "Third World radicals" to transfer funds from weapons procurement in the North to development assistance in the South. As the leader of Canada's delegation to the conference, I negotiated with the president, Muchkund Dubey, a distinguished Indian economist, to find a way to legitimize the disarmament-development relationship. The conference played itself out without any transfer of funds, of course, but the consensus final document said that the two themes were pillars on which enduring international peace and security could be built: "Security consists of not only military but also political, economic, social, humanitarian and human rights and ecological aspects."

This forward-minded definition of security was certainly not embraced by the Western countries, who accelerated their military spending during the Cold War years while, with the exception of the Scandinavian countries, never coming near Pearson's 0.7 per cent target for official development assistance. But an array of high-level commissions at that time was beginning to forge within the consciousness of the international community the idea that it took more than the barrel of a gun to produce security. Willy Brandt, former Chancellor of West Germany, Olof Palme, former Prime Minister of Sweden, and Gro Harlem Brundtland, former Prime Minister of Norway, led teams of thinkers who laid the groundwork for a new understanding of common security. Strong militaries, impressive economic growth numbers, and the continued domination of international policies by the rich countries of the North were only leading to more division and turmoil, they said. This was a fertile period in the development of the modern world, and the prescient words of these pioneers of what might be called "globalization with a conscience" are borne out today in the democratization of Latin America, the Arab Spring, the Occupy movement, and other challenges to the existing elitist hold on power.

HUMAN SECURITY INDEX

Political wisdom slowly began to crystallize as the 1990s arrived, and not the least of those responsible was the modest and utterly charming Pakistani economist Mahbub ul Haq, who turned the tables on his fellow economists. Educated at what he called the "Western citadels of learning" of Cambridge, Yale, and Harvard in the 1950s, he rejected the "tacit assumption" in economics that the real purpose of development was to increase national income. He was branded an economic heretic for calling for more sophisticated measurements, such as life expectancy, education, and welfare as well as wealth. I met Mahbub at meetings of the North-South Roundtable, a group of development practitioners and writers, which worked for many years on priority areas for development: food, energy, technology, transfer of resources, and the elimination of absolute poverty. By this time, Mahbub was an adviser to the World Bank and I considered him a mentor, as I did author and *Economist* editor Barbara Ward, who wrote movingly of the need to improve "stewardship of this beautiful, subtle, incredibly delicate, fragile planet."

Mahbub joined UNDP and it was there that he became accepted as one of the visionaries of international development. He started the *Human Development Report* in 1990 with the simply stated premise that has guided the subsequent annual reports: "People are the real wealth of a nation." The publication's fame is probably more attributable to the index of the most liveable countries it contains each year. Countries are ranked on education, health, housing, and a number of social standards, a way Mahbub devised of graphically showing that when these criteria are neglected or under-funded, the country can be seen to be a desperate place to live. For years, Canada was in the top rank, and when it slipped, opposition parliamentarians criticized the government, ignoring completely the primary idea behind the human security index, which is to put a spotlight on glaring deficiencies in Southern countries rather than to ensure that the rich countries are kept in their comfort zones.

Working closely with Amartya Sen — an Indian economist who in 1998, the year of Mahbub's death, was awarded the Nobel Prize in Economics — Mahbub showed that the basic purpose of development is to enlarge people's choices. "People often value achievements that do not show up at all, or not immediately, in income or growth figures: greater access to knowledge, better nutrition and health services, more secure livelihoods, security against crime and physical violence, satisfying leisure hours, political and cultural freedoms and sense of participation in community activities," he wrote.

Even though the Western governments persisted in separating the business of arms and warfare from economic and social development (always finding money for wars they deemed necessary to fight while keeping aid budgets low), Mahbub's steady insistence that sustainable development is a multi-layered process began to take hold.

In 2000, the UN set out a series of time-bound targets for development, ranging from halving the 1990 extreme poverty rate to putting all children through primary school by 2015; these were combined to form the Millennium Development Goals. The eight goals are to eradicate extreme poverty and hunger; to achieve universal primary education; to promote gender equality and empower women; to reduce child mortality; to improve maternal health; to combat HIV/AIDS, malaria, and other diseases; to ensure environmental sustainability; and to develop a global partnership for development. Twenty-seven UN and related agencies pooled their strengths to advance this far-flung agenda and in 2012 (three years before the target date) reported that the 1990 poverty rate had already been halved. The world has also met the target of halving the proportion of people without access to clean water; between 1990 and 2010, two billion people gained access to improved drinking water sources, such as piped supplies and protected wells. More people have housing and sanitation. Maternal health has improved and fewer children are dying in the early years. More children are in school, with girls benefitting the most from this increase. The report is not all good: Hunger remains a global challenge, the number of people living in slums continues to grow, gender inequality persists, and women continue to face discrimination in access to education, work and economic assets, and participation in government.

It is sometimes said that if China, with its overwhelming population numbers, is removed from the Millennium Development Goals calculus, the results would not be so impressive. But the *2013 Human Development Report* shows that more than forty developing countries have made greater human development gains in recent decades than would have been predicted. These gains are attributable to sustained investment in education, health care, and social programs, which was precisely Mahbub's point.

A few months after our conversation, Helen Clark journeyed to Mexico City to stand beside Mexican President Enrique Peña Nieto in launching the report, which was called *The Rise of the South: Human Progress in a Diverse World*. "The South as a whole," she told the gathering, "is driving global economic growth and societal change for the first time in centuries." She then detailed some of the changes: China and India doubled per capita economic output in less than twenty years — a rate twice as fast as that of European and North American countries during the Industrial Revolution. By 2020, the combined output of the three leading South economies — China, India, and Brazil — will surpass the aggregate production of Canada, France, Germany, Italy, the UK, and the US. Mobile phones with Internet links are now found in most households in Asia, Latin America, and in much of Africa — and most of those affordable smart phones are produced by South-based companies. Brazil, China, India, Indonesia, and Mexico have more daily social media traffic than any country except the US.

NO DEVELOPMENT WITHOUT SECURITY

The advances in human development are most pronounced in countries that have not seen wars or civil conflicts in the past decade. Put another way, the countries farthest from achieving the Millennium Development Goals are the fragile states that have endured recent wars and violent conflict. Sustainable development cannot occur when people are violently uprooted by war (let alone killed or maimed). That unassailable fact should be trumpeted. It is so elementary a fact that it should dominate the UN agenda. UN Secretary-General Ban Ki-moon has spoken out, criticizing high expenditures on arms, particularly nuclear weapons, that come at the expense of fully achieving the Millennium Development Goals. "No development, no peace," he said.

"No disarmament, no security. Yet when both advance, the world advances, with increased security and prosperity for all." Still, most of the UN tiptoes around this subject. Periodic reviews of the Millennium Development Goals tread lightly, even though violence in its many forms against women continues to undermine efforts to reach all the goals.

Many UN conferences on social problems could deal with this subject but hesitate to stir up the old fires, as doing so would surely draw a scolding from the Northern powers. The permanent militarization of the US with its powerful military-industrial complex dominates political thinking in the UN's headquarters in New York. The lessons of the fractious disarmament-development conference have produced a reticence to overtly call, in the name of good governance if not sanity itself, for less money to be devoted to militarism in all its aspects and more to improving people's lives. Stronger security for all would result.

While I am critical of the political process, which has, for the most part, given up on the old idea of moving money from guns to butter, I recognize that new ideas may succeed in making what we often call the downtrodden countries more equitable places to live. A new approach, which UNDP exemplifies, fuses development, human rights, and human security into a new basis for peace. The UN Intellectual History Project regards this as a momentous development: "The integration of these important facets of the human challenge may be the most significant intellectual achievement of the world organization." We can see the hand of Mahbub ul Haq in this, and certainly Helen Clark's, but also the foresight of Kofi Annan, the former Secretary-General, as well as the world commissions of the 1990s, all of whom contributed greatly to enlarging our understanding of true human security.

When the sixtieth anniversary of the UN was approaching in 2005, Kofi Annan presented a report, *In Larger Freedom*, drawing on "my own conscience and convictions" to guide countries.

The notion of larger freedom, he said, "encapsulates the idea that development, security and human rights go hand in hand." The reinforcing nature of these themes needs to be emphasized in the new era of rapid technological advances, he said. "We will not enjoy development without security, we will not enjoy security without development, and we will not enjoy either without respect for human rights." Page after page of Annan's report called for the international community to take action on a dozen fronts, such as investment priorities, debt, trade, environmental sustainability, science and technology for development, and a comprehensive strategy to end global terrorism.

These words and the work of a high-level panel Annan set up doubtless influenced the leaders of the world when they assembled at the UN for the sixtieth anniversary. They issued a declaration stating that many threats are interlinked and that development, peace, and human rights are mutually reinforcing, and showed the growth in political understanding of security by affirming: "Peace and security, development and human rights are the pillars of the United Nations system and the foundations for collective security and well-being." This groundbreaking session also introduced the concept of the "responsibility to protect," a theme I will deal with in Chapter 4. Integrating these ideals into the messy business of state sovereignty remains a challenge. At least, they gave a spurt to the forward movement of the Millennium Development Goals, already underway. And they opened the way for the UNDP to move more confidently into fostering development in the conflict-torn zones that came to be called "fragile states," which contain the bulk of the most deprived people on earth.

SPOTLIGHTING FRAGILE STATES

A fragile state is a low-income, poorly administered country where often people are trapped in a vicious cycle of violent conflict and poverty or suffer from natural resource shortages; many, such as the Democratic Republic of Congo, are emerging from multiple crises and cannot deliver even the most basic services to their citizens. Perhaps thirty to forty countries would be called fragile, among them: Afghanistan, Burundi, Central African Republic, Chad, East Timor, Ethiopia, Guinea, Guinea-Bissau, Haiti, Ivory Coast, Liberia, Nepal, Papua New Guinea, Sierra Leone, the Solomon Islands, Somalia, South Sudan, and Togo. Foreign aid has customarily been seen to be less effective in these areas because the states have less capacity to absorb aid, but without aid, their situation will worsen.

Helen Clark sees reaching these people as a chief part of her mission. "Some 1.5 billion people are estimated to live in fragile and conflict-affected states or in countries with very high levels of criminal violence," she told an audience at Oxford University. "That makes promoting peace and security, in the broader sense, critical for securing human development." Nine of the ten countries ranking lowest on the human development index experienced conflict in the past twenty years. In short, conflict jeopardizes development.

To give development a chance, UNDP works with its partners in the UN system to stabilize economic, political, and environmental systems to provide better government. "The work of humanitarian, peacekeeping, and development actors should be mutually reinforcing," Clark said. The object is to ensure that people feel secure enough to invest in their own futures, develop a capacity to engage in conflict resolution and mediation, and rebuild trust between citizens and the state to deal with the legacy of violence. In El Salvador, UNDP helped communities to improve police response times and established gun-free zones in twenty of the most violent municipalities. In South Sudan, UNDP's Community Security and Arms Control Initiative established fifty police stations, giving a greater sense of security to older people and women. In Sudan, UNDP reintegrated former fighters through vocational training, loans to start businesses, and civic education to help them participate in local peace committees in order to reduce the chance that they will be drawn into further conflict. In Somalia, UNDP helped the government establish mobile courts to improve access to judicial services across the country. "Our work is holistic," Clark said in her lecture. "It goes beyond the ex-combatants to focus on reducing armed violence and creating livelihood opportunities."

UNDP has a department dealing with fragile states, which is overseen by former Spanish diplomat Magdy Martinez-Soliman, whom I visited in his office. He was working on the final details of an international dialogue with many development partners and international organizations and including representatives of nineteen fragile and conflict-affected states. "The current ways of working in fragile states needs serious improvement," he said. "Transitioning out of fragility is long political work that requires country leadership and ownership. Processes of political dialogue have often failed due to lack of trust, inclusiveness, and leadership." So he is guiding a program called the "New Deal for Engagement in Fragile States," with the empowerment of women, youth, and marginalized groups as key actors for peacebuilding. The "New Deal" is setting goals for peacebuilding in the fragile states and emphasizes strengthening the capacities of the affected countries by helping the authorities focus on improving political settlements, establishing better security, addressing injustices, generating employment, and becoming more accountable in delivering social services.

Development has come a long way since the 0.7 per cent target was introduced more than four decades ago. Foreign aid was then an isolated endeavour. Today, the whole UN system is moving to fuller involvement in dealing with conflict in fragile states as a way of shoring up the development process and doing this in a way that does not jab elbows at the military. This is the agenda that Helen Clark is pushing forward.

A POST-2015 DEVELOPMENT AGENDA

Her main vehicle is the report issued by a future-oriented team of experts representing fifty UN entities and operating under the unwieldy title of the UN System Task Team on the Post-2015 UN Development Agenda. When the team began work in early 2012, she challenged them to take development forward from the Millennium Development Goal targets.

"The post-2015 agenda that follows the Millennium Development Goals will have to be even more ambitious," she told the group when it met in South Africa. "In seeking to build a better future for all, we will have to concentrate on human rights, democracy, and good governance as intrinsic to development. We're hearing an increasing demand from civil society to discuss ways of including government and accountability in the global development agenda, both to ensure the legitimacy of development policies and essential to extending human dignity and justice." Honest and responsive government, along with education, are top priorities. While education, clean water, and health services remain important issues, human development also requires attention to the global jobs crisis, growing inequality, natural resource scarcities, and climate change in order to deal with peace and security, Clark said.

The group took up her challenge and its final report foresaw the eradication of extreme poverty throughout the world by 2030. "We envision a world in 2030 where no person has been left behind, and where there are schools, clinics and clean water for all. It is a world where there are jobs for young people, where businesses thrive, and where we have brought patterns of consumption and production into balance." *The Economist* was so impressed with the work it featured the forecast on its cover with the banner "Towards the End of Poverty."

The Post-2015 planners backed up their rosy view with charts, statistics, and a lot of conviction that governments, international organizations, civil society, businesses, and foundations would act on this "bold and ambitious vision" and make the most of this transformative moment in history.

Their major qualification came towards the end of the report with the admonition "Peace and justice are prerequisites for progress." The group warned that without peace, children could not go to school or access health clinics. Adults could not go to their workplaces and markets or cultivate their fields. Conflict could unravel years, even decades, of social and economic progress in a brief time. "The character of violence has shifted dramatically in the past few decades. Contemporary conflict is characterized by the blurring of boundaries . . . and the targeting of civilian populations. Violence, drugs and arms spill rapidly across borders in our increasingly connected world." They argued that the greatest danger arises when weak institutions are unable to deal with these tensions and thus the pace of development inevitably depends on stronger institutions for conflict resolution and mediation. They hit home the new argument for establishing the relationship between disarmament and development:

"To achieve peace, leaders must tackle the problems that matter most to people: they must prosecute corruption and unlawful violence, especially against minorities and vulnerable groups. They must enhance accountability. They must prove that the state can deliver basic services and rights, such as access to safety and justice, safe drinking water and health services, without discrimination."

The 2030 vision is not just rhetoric. It involves stabilizing commodity prices so that the poorest nations get a fair share of profits; effectively dealing with international corruption, organized crime, and the illicit trade in persons; and severely reducing the flow of arms across borders. What struck me most about the report was its sureness that all this could be accomplished. While it will be unquestionably harder to lift another billion people out of poverty by 2030 than it was to lift up the billion between 2000 and 2015, the group found itself energized by the prospect of "a global partnership for a people-centred and planet-sensitive agenda based on the principle of our common humanity." A better world is clearly within reach.

The UNDP can do all the planning it wants, but it is up to the UN's member states to implement the new ideas, a point made by the General Assembly president, John W. Ashe of the twin-island Caribbean nation of Antigua and Barbuda, who challenged his colleagues to "find the common ground as a basis for moving forward with decisive action."

This planning for the future lying just over the horizon is the United Nations at its best. The UNDP is trying to repair the damages of today and, at the same time, chart a course leading to a stronger humanity tomorrow. Very careful political leadership is required, for the rich nations will not easily give up their self-assumed prerogatives in trade and finance. The shoals are formidable. One statistic, above all, shows the inequity that still plagues the world, despite the progress in development: The 1.2 billion poorest people today account for only 1 per cent of world consumption while the billion richest consume 72 per cent. Thanks to the UNDP, the voices of the poorest are starting to be heard.

Who can say what upheavals are ahead caused by the growing concentration of wealth at the top of the income ladder in the industrialized countries and even many of the countries of the South, including China and India? Or by climate change, which is already causing storms, floods, and droughts of unprecedented magnitude? Or by resource scarcities, including water shortages, sure to stir more conflict? As Yogi Berra put it, "The future ain't what it used to be."

Former US Vice-President Al Gore has discerned the most

important drivers of global change in his book *The Future*. These include economic growth, communications, pollution, technology, and power balances. In first place he put the emergence of a deeply interconnected global economy "that increasingly operates as a fully integrated holistic entity," drawing in those areas of the world that during the twentieth century were outside the mainstream decision-making processes. The UN Security Council and the international financial institutions, such as the World Bank and the International Monetary Fund, are prime examples of how the West dominated world politics and finances. Already, the twenty-first century has seen the emergence of a new group of states demanding their share of power: the BRICS. This enticing acronym stands for Brazil, Russia, India, China, and South Africa, which, as major emergent market economies, have opened their own development bank, challenging the old institutions. These are the states predicted to lead world growth. But even they will not be able to attain more sustainable patterns of consumption and production and resource use by themselves. Persistent inequalities and struggles over scarce resources will plague all nations unless there is a global compact to deal with universal problems: conflict, hunger, insecurity, and violence.

Development visionaries, stimulated by the Post-2015 report, want to move development forward for all and have set priorities for a more holistic approach: inclusive social development, inclusive economic development, environmental sustainability, and peace and security. This last priority shows that conflict, violence, and disaster are no longer marginal issues in global development discourse, and thus better mechanisms to reduce violence and foster sustainable peace are essential. The global partnership for development that Helen Clark seeks must include ways to protect people from violence and give them a chance to live their lives in dignity.

CHAPTER 4:
The UN and the Responsibility to Protect

The United Nations Operations and Crisis Center, operating behind locked doors on the seventh floor of the UN Secretariat Building in New York, is staffed by a specially trained team of young officers working in twelve-hour shifts around the clock. There's no such thing as no one to answer the phone when a crisis erupts in some zone of conflict and a field officer needs direct contact and instructions from headquarters, as has happened in the past. The soul-wrenching genocides in Srebrenica and Rwanda, which blotted the reputation of the UN in the 1990s because the organization did not respond with sufficient speed, are unlikely to occur again, at least where the UN has a presence.

When I visited the Center in April 2013, Mali, a land-locked country of fifteen million people in West Africa, was on everyone's minds. The Security Council needed updates on the situation on the ground where fighting between Islamist rebels and Mali and French troops had raged for months. Whether to send a UN peacekeeping mission into a zone of conflict still had to be decided. Two weeks later, the Council authorized a force of 12,600 troops "to use all necessary means" to enforce security, including the protection of civilians, humanitarian aid, UN staff, and cultural artefacts. The UN troops stopped virtually all the fighting. By September, elections had been held and a new president, Ibrahim Boubacar Keita, installed in a peaceful ceremony. The UN Mali mission basically stabilized the country and provided one more example that UN peacekeeping works — when the five veto-wielding permanent members of the Security Council allow it. The world heard little about the UN success in Mali, but plenty about the UN failure to stop the killing in Syria. Why is the UN successful in some areas and not in others?

THE HEART OF UN PEACE OPERATIONS

The focal point of the Operations and Crisis Center is the Watch Room, divided into a dozen cubicles where operators, usually handling two computers at once and backed up by a battery of TV monitors, deal in real-time communication with the UN's peace-keeping forces and political missions. At present there are sixteen peacekeeping missions, mostly in African and Middle Eastern countries, deploying more than one hundred thousand troops. An additional thirteen political missions deal with a diversity of development and human rights issues.

I commented to Ian Sinclair, a former British military officer who commands the Center, that the atmosphere seemed quite calm despite turmoil in a lot of places. "These are professionals in here," he said, "but it can get a little hectic at five o'clock in the morning when the staff starts to assemble the daily summary product. We paint a picture, with graphs and maps, of what is happening in key places in terms of politics, security, humanitarian issues, and human rights in the previous twenty-four hours. Also, we support crisis management in which headquarters responds to problems. We help to connect specialists in the field with their counterparts here." The "product" this day dealt with the latest events in Sudan and Bangladesh as well as Mali. The team also keeps a close eye on Burundi, Sierra Leone,

Guinea-Bissau, and the Central African Republic, all post-conflict countries going through reconstruction.

Attached to the Watch Room are crisis rooms, again outfitted with the latest communications technologies, where senior UN personnel gather three times a week for verbal briefings by Sinclair. He was seconded to the UN after tours in Afghanistan and Cyprus where he was chief-of-staff at the long-running peacekeeping force separating the Turkish and Cypriot militaries. He stayed on at the UN as a civilian. "I'm still doing a little something for good in the world," he told me, with a dry British understatement. "I like what peacekeeping does. It's low-cost and it's effective. You can keep the lid on little, and not so-little, brush-fires around the world."

UN Peacekeeping Forces, awarded the Nobel Peace Prize in 1988, have been at the heart of UN peace operations since 1948. Sixty-seven operations have been conducted in forty-two countries over the course of six and a half decades. Peacekeeping operations in Cambodia, El Salvador, Liberia, Mozambique, Namibia, and Sierra Leone stand out as success stories.

More than 3,100 UN peacekeeping personnel have died in the line of duty and $90 billion has been spent on the entire enterprise. European and Canadian troop contributions have sharply declined in recent years; in 2012, 85 per cent of UN peacekeepers were Asian or African in origin.

Peacekeeping remains a critical element of a broader international peace and security architecture. It is a very versatile tool but also cost effective. The resources spent by the international community on UN peacekeeping are but a small fraction of global defence spending. Despite the relatively low price tag, a credible body of research credits peacekeeping with contributing significantly to the decline in casualties due to civil wars. The investment in peacekeeping has also prevented and alleviated suffering for an untold number of people. The relative stability peacekeeping offers has also helped restore local and international investors' confidence in post-conflict zones, increasing economic activity and raising the GDP of these same countries. Put plainly, peacekeeping works.

Though it started out as a communications hub for peace-keeping forces in the field, the Crisis Center developed into a crossroads where the main branches of the UN's peace work all intersect and exchange information. The three pillars of security — peacekeeping, development, and human rights — are all involved. The daily product of information fuses the work and observations of these three pillars.

INTEGRATING UN OPERATIONS

This is the new UN, working in integrated, holistic ways. It still can do only what the major powers will let it. The inability of the UN to resolve the crisis in Syria is not the fault of the UN itself, but rather that of the major powers, who agreed only on sending inspectors to clear chemical weapons out of Syria but could not agree on how to intervene to stop the civil-war bloodshed.

The UN has suffered greatly in struggling to play the role that the founders envisioned when they wrote in the Charter that the Security Council held "primary responsibility for the mainten-ance of international peace and security." The power struggles among the five major powers of the Security Council — the US, Russia, China, the United Kingdom, and France, each possessing a veto — have often immobilized the UN.

When the UN came into existence in 1945, the five major pow-ers at the time each gave themselves a veto over any matter the Security Council would deal with. These countries would likely not have joined the UN without such a power. Over the years, well over two hundred vetoes on substantive issues have been cast. The most recent instances have been the US veto in 2011 of a resolution condemning Israeli settlements in the West Bank.

In 2012, China and Russia vetoed two resolutions threatening to use military force in Syria to stop the conflict. In the past, vetoes have been cast to block the admission of member states and the election of a Secretary-General. The veto is a relic of the past, but the UN seems stuck with it: The major powers have a veto over removal of the veto. Efforts to reform the composition of the permanent membership of the council — Germany, Brazil, India, and Japan have the strongest cases for membership — have floundered, with states in various regions competing over who should be selected. Meanwhile, most of the world continues to compete for election to two-year terms on the fifteen-member Council — without, of course, veto power.

It is a sad comment on the state of modern democracy that an anachronism dating back to the Second World War prevents the Security Council from truly living up to its mandate to maintain international peace and security. The genocides of Rwanda and Srebrenica can be laid squarely at the doorstep of the big states, which through the years have kept the UN in penury (compared to what these states spend on arms). The UN has never been allowed to mount a standing emergency force capable of being deployed on twenty-four hours' notice to a region where violence is flaring. For years, its peacekeeping forces were restricted in their actions to merely ensuring that a truce between combatants would stick, not actually enforcing the peace with arms. UN Peacekeeping has had to find its way into peacemaking, and there is still hesitation about whether UN forces should, if necessary, actually fight for peace, as the Syria case showed. The UN failures to stop bloodshed have been burnished in the minds of its critics. Yet the mandate to enforce peace in Mali essentially worked.

Despite the obstacles, the UN is moving ahead, and its new strategies are gathering the strength of its far-flung parts into a more coherent instrument for peace. The UN is far better equipped than it used to be, and if it is true that the one who writes the agenda has unseen power, then the UN is becoming more powerful. It is writing the daily agenda of democratic state-building and human development in dozens of countries, notably across the Sahel region of Africa, that are usually not in the news. It has assumed a responsibility to protect people who are oppressed either by their own rulers or by outside forces.

A COMPREHENSIVE AGENDA FOR PEACE

Jan Eliasson, a tall and imposing Swedish diplomat I first met when he came to the UN as ambassador in 1988, embodies the new integration. His solid academic and diplomatic background includes being adviser to Olof Palme — Sweden's Prime Minister who broke ground in the 1980s with his report on common security — and UN mediator in the Iran-Iraq war. Eliasson is Deputy Secretary-General of the UN, a post he has elevated from its normal administrative functions to a role of thinker-in-chief. "Development, peace and security, and human rights are interlinked and mutually reinforcing," he said in his Dag Hammarskjöld Lectures, admitting that the record of these three pillars all working together is not yet very impressive. Emphasizing the rule of law, he says, can have a binding effect. He is pushing to underlay the integrated approach with new approaches to justice in conflict-torn areas. "By prosecuting perpetrators, we begin the process of healing. By facilitating truth and reconciliation, we allow communities to reunite. By fostering reparation and restitution, we plant the seeds for economic growth and empowerment."

Eliasson received me in his office on the thirty-eighth floor. We recalled earlier days when we both served under Secretary-General Javier Pérez de Cuéllar, who gave me a bound copy of the UN Charter in its six official languages.

"Now the world has to deal with problems unforeseen by the charter," I said.

"Yes," Eliasson responded, "but we have new insights into

the inter-relationship of complex elements of planetary exist-ence. If we now combine, in the right way, peace and security with development and human rights, we can establish a more stable international order. All these are mutually reinforcing or mutually damaging."

He spoke quite diplomatically about the need for states to choose to work in a multilateral manner. In fact, he added, good international co-operation enhances national interests.

"Can the UN advance a comprehensive international agenda?" I asked.

"We have the means to organize ourselves well," he said, "and if the UN member states can identify an international role as being in their national interests, then we are certainly on the right course."

"The work of the UN in the Western world is under-appreciated if not unknown," I said. "The financial support of the UN is far less than it should be and, related to military spending, is appalling. How can the UN improve the culture of understanding of the true value of the organization?"

"Well," he responded, "most people today realize they cannot divorce themselves from the world outside. We must provide a message that the world outside must be constantly taken into account. Unfortunately, today the reputation of the UN is influ-enced by the Syria crisis, where there is powerlessness because of the divisions inside the Security Council. This pains the Secretary-General and me and our colleagues, but when I go out into the field, and I have spent a lot of time in the field, I am encouraged."

He reached into his pocket to show me a unique business card he uses which, instead of introducing himself, details what the UN does for humanity every day in providing food, environ-ment, and peacekeeping services. "That's a pretty good business card," I said.

"It's a reminder of our daily work and also those who have

given their lives in the service of the UN," he responded. "I think if you scratch the surface of every world citizen, they have their dreams and aspirations for a strong United Nations. It just takes some reminders that no country is an island, that we need this organization to better our lives. On the other hand, we on the inside of the organization need to realize that institutions have not delivered to the extent people hoped for and expected."

He said the evidence is piling up that environmental, migration, development, and organized-crime problems cannot be solved in isolation. "I'm driving myself and our team to work horizontally, break down borders, and see the beauty of co-operation."

THE FUTURE OF INTERNATIONAL LAW

Comprehensive solutions to the problems of war and development are not particularly new at the UN. In 1987, Perez de Cuellar called for a Comprehensive Global Watch system to monitor the major threats to human security. In 1988, Prime Minister Rajiv Gandhi of India came to the UN to propose a fifteen-year plan for the complete elimination of nuclear weapons. That same year, Mikhail Gorbachev electrified delegates in the General Assembly by calling for an end to the threat or use of force in foreign policy and suggesting a range of new international institutions: a multilateral centre for lessening the dangers of war, an international verification mechanism under UN auspices, a tribunal to investigate acts of terrorism, a special fund for humanitarian co-operation, a world space organization, and a "world consultative council of the world's intellectual elite." Soon after, Gorbachev fell from power with the end of the Cold War, and no subsequent leader in Russia or anywhere else has set out such a stunning panorama.

Instead of blossoming with the end of the Cold War, the UN went into decline with the energy for development of a global security system, it seemed, sapped out of political leaders. Any thought of trust between Russia and the West was blown away when NATO began its months-long bombardment of Serbia and Kosovo in 1999 without Security Council authorization. In the Canadian Senate, I opposed the bombing and was myself attacked by those who felt the bombing was necessary to end the horrible ethnic cleansing perpetrated by the Slobodan Milošević regime in Serbia. When former US President Jimmy Carter expressed his criticism of the NATO campaign, US policy began to shift. But the damage was done. Under cover of retaliation for Serbian barbarism against the Kosovars, NATO was able to obscure the real issue: the future of international law.

The slaughter of innocent people in Kosovo, like similar horrors in Rwanda, Somalia, and Cambodia, must be stopped by military force if necessary but only when authorized by the UN Security Council. There are times when the use of force may be legitimate in the pursuit of peace, but unless the Security Council conducts itself responsibly as the sole source of legitimacy on the use of force, anarchy is bound to result. When the major powers exercise their veto in the council, chaos results, a flaw that has persisted right into the Syrian crisis of 2013. Finally, in the Kosovo case, the council was able to agree on an international military and civilian presence "under United Nations auspices" to end the war and keep the peace. When 9/11 occurred, fear drove the political processes into anti-terrorist overdrive at the expense of the major steps needed to build global security. And the US invasion of Iraq in 2003 dealt another blow to efforts to build global security.

THE RESPONSIBILITY TO PROTECT TAKES HOLD

In this climate it is all the more remarkable that the idea of "the responsibility to protect" survived and is now the basis for a range of UN expanded actions as we come up on 2015, the seventieth anniversary of the UN.

The Kosovo massacres and horrific brutalities in East Timor, when the latter country attempted to break away from Indonesian control, triggered an international debate on whether the international community could ever intervene in states that fail to protect their own peoples or, worse, are themselves the perpetrators of acts of genocide. Which takes precedence: the sovereign power of states or the rights of individuals within those states? Secretary-General Kofi Annan went to the podium of the General Assembly in 2000 to challenge the international community to develop an international norm for intervention to protect civilians from wholesale slaughter.

Canadian Foreign Minister Lloyd Axworthy took up that challenge and established the International Commission on Intervention and State Sovereignty, a body of fifteen experts who, in 2001, issued a report, *The Responsibility to Protect*. Axworthy called the report "a revolutionary document." "It advances the idea that sovereignty is based on the ability and willingness of governments to accept the responsibility to protect their own citizens. Failing that, the international community has a right to intervene." The commission sidestepped the contentious question of when states had a "right" to intervene in other states by framing the issue as a state's "responsibility to protect" its citizens.

The 2005 UN World Summit of one hundred fifty government leaders unanimously endorsed the Responsibility to Protect, stating that the international community, through the United Nations, has the responsibility to use appropriate diplomatic, humanitarian, and other peaceful means to help protect populations from atrocities, and also that collective military action can be taken on a case-by-case basis under the authority of the Security Council if peaceful means are inadequate. The Responsibility to Protect is not about human rights violations or conflict situations in general or even about other humanitarian catastrophes. Rather, it is about responding to four designated crimes: genocide, war crimes, ethnic cleansing, and crimes against humanity.

Three pillars hold the new doctrine together: The first pillar identifies the state as the primary bearer of the responsibility to protect populations from mass atrocities; the second establishes the responsibility of the international community to assist states in protecting populations; the third defines the responsibility of the international community to intervene by taking collective action in a timely manner in accordance with the UN charter. It is often thought that the purpose of the Responsibility to Protect is to permit the use of force. While force is permitted as a last resort, there is a wide range of prior options, including preventive diplomacy, fact-finding missions, economic sanctions and embargoes, and military operations, such as no-fly zones, monitoring, and civilian defence missions.

A textbook example of the care needed to exercise the Responsibility to Protect is Libya, where Colonel Muammar Gaddafi responded to peaceful protests against the excesses of his regime by massacring several hundred of his own people. When Gaddafi ignored a Security Council demand that attacks against civilians stop and threatened to wipe out the rebel stronghold of Benghazi, the council invoked the Responsibility to Protect and authorized military intervention to protect civilians. NATO commenced action immediately. A furious but short war followed. It ended when Gaddafi was killed by fighters who captured him in his hometown of Sirte. Many exulted that the Responsibility to Protect had worked; others criticized NATO for exceeding the mandate of the Security Council by carrying out "regime change." When the Responsibility to Protect principles were first struck, the emphasis was on the protection of innocent people, not necessarily winning a war, much less violently deposing the ruler of the country. How far to go in implementing the Responsibility to Protect remains a contentious question. If the powerful states insist that the principles include ousting an abhorred dictator, then it may become impossible to get Security Council agreement on further use of military force in situations where atrocious crimes are being committed. The long impasse over Security Council action on Syria illustrates this point.

The Ivory Coast offers another example of the Responsibility to Protect in action, with a less disputatious outcome. Following presidential elections in 2010, violence broke out, resulting in high civilian death tolls and massive displacement. The international community responded rapidly with economic sanctions and calls for political reform. As the conflict escalated with widespread mass atrocities, the UN Security Council unanimously voted to strengthen the UN mission on the ground to protect the civilian population.

In Kenya, when a disputed presidential election in 2007 triggered violence, the African Union stepped in and mediated a power-sharing agreement. This was praised as a model of diplomatic action under the Responsibility to Protect by several civil society organizations.

In Guinea in 2009, government forces interrupted a peaceful political protest in a stadium in Conakry, opened fire on civilians, and committed widespread sexual violence and rape, amounting to crimes against humanity. The Economic Community of West African States and the African Union rapidly initiated a mediation effort and imposed economic sanctions, measures that quickly led to the formation of a unity government. A political solution prevented more conflict.

In other places, the Responsibility to Protect has had less impressive results. Remnants of the war in Congo linger, despite international efforts to implement a peace process. The deadliest war in modern African history, it directly involved nine African nations, as well as about twenty armed groups, and killed 5.4 million people, mostly from disease and starvation. Crimes against humanity and war crimes against civilian populations — including murder, rape and sexual slavery, recruitment of child soldiers, and forced displacement — continued for years. In Darfur, the Sudanese government responded to a rebellion in 2003, killing three hundred thousand people and displacing three million in a conflict extending more than ten years. There have never been enough African Union and UN peace forces in the area.

Claiming that Western forces over-reached the Security Council mandate in Libya, a number of important states, notably including the BRICS (Brazil, Russia, India, China, and South Africa), are apprehensive about future Security Council mandates for the Responsibility to Protect. The way the US, UK, and France have conflated the protection of innocent civilians with regime change makes others nervous that a new form of Western imperialism secretly underlies the supposed good intentions. This has led Gareth Evans — former Australian Foreign Minister and co-chairman of the commission that established the Responsibility to Protect — to campaign anew for the original principles, centering on clear-cut criteria and strict monitoring. I interviewed Evans by email for his views of whether a matured understanding of the Responsibility to Protect could find a formula for the international community to rely on.

"Can the Responsibility to Protect effectively stop human slaughters and other deranged behaviours without necessarily toppling the government and banishing (when not assassinating) the leadership?" I asked him.

"While I acknowledge that there are going to be some Responsibility to Protect cases where civilian protection can be achieved only by full-scale regime change, I'm not persuaded that this is always going to be necessary, even in cases of protracted civil war or mass insurrection," he said. "Certainly, it's very hard to justify the NATO position in this respect in Libya: A big mistake was made by the US, the UK, and France in not taking seriously the ceasefire and peace proposal initiatives that came from Gaddafi and the South Africans as the intervention went on. If the objective really was civilian protection, that should have been fully explored. Failure to observe the distinction contributed hugely to the paralysis since over Syria."

Evans says that a fine line has to be walked politically to achieve an effective and supportable response to atrocities. He lays down five questions that must be answered in each case: Does the scale of the human rights abuse justify the use of force? Is the primary purpose of the proposed military action to halt or avert the threat in question? Has every non-military option been fully explored? Is the scale of the military action the minimum necessary? Will those at risk ultimately be better or worse off? The lack of trust between the major powers themselves and, indeed, between much of the South and the powerful states of the North generates endless wrangling. Nonetheless, says Evans, "the Responsibility to Protect principle is firmly and globally established and has demonstrably delivered major practical results, but its completely effective implementation is going to be a work in progress for a long time yet."

In response to the controversial implementation of the Responsibility to Protect in Libya, Brazil introduced a document on "Responsibility While Protecting," which calls for greater accountability and clarity of purpose when R2P norms are being implemented, including the kinds of precautionary questions Evans suggests. Developing the "normative framework" for implementing the Responsibility to Protect will be an essential aspect of strengthening the UN's peace and security functions in the years ahead.

INTERNATIONAL CRIMINAL COURT

Just as the Responsibility to Protect doctrine reflects humanity's growing sense of stewardship in global development, so too the inauguration of the International Criminal Court in 2002 puts some teeth in punishing perpetrators of war crimes. Situated in The Hague and supported by 122 states (a long way from universality, especially since the US, Russia, and China don't belong), the court is an outgrowth of the special tribunals that prosecuted war criminals in the former Yugoslavia and Rwanda. The history of prosecuting war criminals goes back to the Nuremburg and Tokyo trials following the Second World War. The new independent, permanent court tries persons accused of the most serious crimes of genocide, crimes against humanity, and war crimes.

In its first decade, sixteen cases came before the court from African states: Uganda, the Democratic Republic of Congo, the Central African Republic, Darfur (Sudan), Kenya, Libya, and Ivory Coast. Investigations have started in Afghanistan, Colombia, Georgia, Honduras, Nigeria, South Korea, Guinea, and Mali. The court convicted Congolese warlord Thomas Lubanga Dyilo and sentenced him to fourteen years' imprisonment for "conscripting and enlisting children under the age of fifteen years and using them to participate actively in hostilities." Rebels under his command committed massive human rights violations, including ethnic massacres, murder, torture, rape, and mutilation.

Since there was only one conviction in the first decade, the court's teeth might not seem sharp. The first person indicted, Joseph Kony — the Lord's Resistance Army leader in Uganda accused of thirty-three counts of war crimes, including murder, rape, sexual enslavement, using child soldiers, and inhumane acts — has escaped capture for many years because the court did not have sufficient means to apprehend him. Legal experts think the court may not hit its stride until its second or third decade. It stretches credulity to think that war criminals are only to be found in benighted countries, yet Western countries for the most part are resisting involvement in the International Criminal Court. And efforts to label the use of nuclear weapons a crime against humanity were thwarted by the major powers. Meanwhile, at least war criminals' comfort in impunity has been severely challenged by the growing reach of the new court.

PREVENTION OF GENOCIDE

Heading off atrocities before they start is the work of a new UN office, Prevention of Genocide, charged with mobilizing action in troubled areas before mass killings begin. This work of prevention — distinct from cleanup after slaughters — may become the most important contribution the UN makes to building peace in the twenty-first century. If atrocities do not break out in such strife-torn areas as the Central African Republic, Congo, Myanmar, Guinea, Nigeria, and Sudan — areas now under investigation — credit may belong to the quiet, forward-minded work of the Prevention of Genocide office. Its accomplishments will likely never be in headlines, and the world will go on oblivious to prevention. It is the tragedies that make the news.

The genocidal violence in Rwanda and the Balkans spurred the UN to open an office in 2007 dedicated to averting future such calamities. Its current director, Adama Dieng, an international law expert from Senegal, was appointed in July 2012. A few months after he took over, I went to see Dieng, whose quarters in a building near the UN are behind locked doors. Dieng graduated in international law from the Hague Academy of International Law and worked his way through a number of legal posts before becoming Registrar of the International Tribunal for Rwanda. Lanky, with greying hair, he speaks softly, and I had to strain to hear him as he described the experiences that brought him to his present post.

"I left Rwanda two days before the genocide started," he said. "I was the last official to deal with the government. God knows,

I might not be here today if I had not left immediately. Perhaps 800,000 people who were killed could have been saved if the international community had had an early warning system in place. After I got out, I was among the first to alert the international community and call on the Human Rights Commission to have a commission of inquiry established."

Later, he presided over the Rwanda tribunal. "I witnessed the suffering of those victims who came to testify before the tribunal. It is extremely important that we remember what happened in Rwanda. We have to stand up and fight against these cruelties. This has led me to believe with all my heart that prevention is the key to making the world a better place."

As the Secretary-General's Special Advisor on the Prevention of Genocide, Dieng is charged with collecting information on massive violations of human rights and international humanitarian law of ethnic and racial origin that might, if not halted, lead to genocide. His reports go to the Security Council, which has the power to act. Thus the genocide prevention adviser acts as an early warning system. His work will be buttressed by the Atrocities Prevention Board, created in the US by President Obama in 2012 to make the deterrence of genocide and mass atrocities "a core national security interest and core moral responsibility."

Dieng's predecessor, Francis Deng, sent a report in 2009 to the Security Council warning that in Congo genocide was a threat due to extreme ethnic polarization and hatred. It took time, but the council eventually set in motion negotiations with the African Union, European Union, and the US to establish an eleven-nation Peace, Security, and Cooperation Framework agreement covering Congo and its neighbours in the Great Lakes region of Africa. With its recurring cycles of violence, Congo has eluded UN peace efforts, but the prospects improved with the appointment of Mary Robinson, former President of Ireland, as the Secretary-General's special envoy, backed up a peace-enforcement brigade of UN troops. The UN force succeeded in getting the rebels to lay down their arms. Genocide has been averted.

Adama Dieng brings to his job a determination to keep the Security Council apprised of reliable information as a first step to action. Shortly after he was appointed, he told the General Assembly, "What is crucial here is that we need to be ready to act and to act effectively when the need arises. And to be effective, the groundwork needs to be done beforehand. We all have a role to play. The Responsibility to Protect calls for each of us — member states, international, regional, and civil society — to protect populations at risk."

When we spoke, his attention was also focused on the crises in Syria and the Central African Republic. Diplomatically, he said it was up to the Security Council to act in Syria; the facts of the killings there were well established. Describing the breakdown of law and order in the Central African Republic, one of the world's poorest countries with a long history of chaos and coups, he said there was still time to prevent atrocities and stop the escalation of rampages by soldiers. He appealed to the Security Council to act. Again it took time, but a year later the council authorized an African Union peacekeeping force to counter rebel soldiers who had been pillaging, raping, and conscripting child soldiers at will.

Taking the long view, Dieng told me that the UN has a wide range of tools — commissions of inquiry, sanctions, special envoys, judicial settlement of disputes, referrals to the International Criminal Court — that can be used to head off future genocides without resorting to force. "Despite ongoing crises, the UN has made real progress. It is now universally recognized that averting future genocides is a shared responsibility, and more nations are becoming involved."

Dag Hammarskjöld first articulated the concept of preventive diplomacy — diplomatic action to prevent disputes from escalating into conflicts — a half century ago. After a long gestation period, it appears to be taken seriously by a growing number of governments. Regional organizations, such as the African Union, have updated their strategies to regularize proactive diplomacy to protect democratic institutions and resolve crises. "Without a doubt," Ban Ki-moon told the General Assembly, "it is one of the smartest investments we can make."

CHAPTER 5:
The Right to Peace Takes Shape

Professor Carlos Villan Duran sat back in his chair and stared out the window for a minute. "I'm not very happy with the results of the workshop today," he said. "I realize that in the United States and other Western countries, many do not share my view on the human right to peace, so their opposition was not a surprise to me. Yet I felt a little frustrated." Duran had been the main speaker at a meeting convened by the University of Notre Dame in Indiana in 2013 to discuss the UN Draft Declaration on the Right of Peoples to Peace. When the day was over, Duran and I talked in my room at the Inn of Saint Mary's, a charming hotel on the edge of the university campus.

It is surprising that just when human rights in their many manifestations have become lodged in most governments' consciousness, the idea that every human being has a right to be free from the ravages of war is so controversial — at least among policy-makers in the West. An effort is under way at the UN to adopt a declaration stating that all individuals have the right to live in peace so that they can develop fully all their capacities — physical, intellectual, moral, and spiritual — without being the target of violence. Such thinking could well result in outlawing war. While this would move humanity to a higher state of existence, the idea is not welcomed by those convinced that peace comes only through the flexing of military muscle. Arms-makers definitely reject the thought.

Duran, who is president of the Spanish Society for International Human Rights Law, is the chief driver of the endeavour, which stems from a resolution adopted by the UN Human Rights Council in 2012 on "promotion of the right to peace." The council prepared a draft declaration, and governments and civil society groups around the world are examining it before it goes to the floor of the General Assembly for a vote in 2014 or 2015. Governments at that time will have to decide if they will abide by a legal obligation to renounce the use or threat of force in international relations, and that their subjects can hold them accountable. "The Notre Dame meeting did not meet our expectations," Duran said simply.

"Are the expectations too high given the atmosphere of the culture of war that still prevails?" I asked. "Society as a whole still thinks in terms of the legitimate use of force as a starting point to get to peace, rather than building the conditions for peace to avoid recourse to militarism."

"I am persuaded that ordinary people are more concerned with enjoying basic human rights, and the first of these is the right to live in peace," he responded. "The hesitations are coming from governments, not the people, and particularly from governments that have strong military power. Yes, there is a culture of violence in society and ordinary people are suffering from this, but they want to get beyond violence."

Duran said that women have a more intuitive understanding of the right to peace than men. "Women have a stronger feeling for peace. Women give birth, they give life, and they do not understand the culture of violence. I am convinced that women can more dramatically advance peace issues. They rather than men are ready to understand and accept what peace means."

As an international lawyer, Duran worked for twenty-three years in the Office of the High Commissioner for Human Rights in the UN's Geneva office. Concerned that his own government of Spain had joined in what he termed "the illegal war in Iraq," he retired from his UN post and founded the Spanish Society for Human Rights Law to work full time, principally with Spanish-speaking countries, drafting a declaration on the right to peace. When the Spanish parliament unanimously accepted an early draft, he felt emboldened to move ahead to seek global accept-ance through the UN.

The opposition he encountered in the Notre Dame workshop was still in his mind, particularly the comments by a US law pro-fessor that states do not need a peace declaration; they could just carry on with "business as usual."

"It's true," Duran said, "some states like the US, Canada, the Netherlands, and the UK think that 'business as usual' is enough to bring peace. That certainly was not the case in Iraq. The old Roman maxim, 'If you want peace, prepare for war,' is no longer valid in today's globalized world where we are all dependent upon one another for our security. All governments must real-ize that the preservation, promotion, and implementation of the right to peace constitute a fundamental obligation."

A GLOBAL ETHIC OF NON-VIOLENCE

The right to peace is not a new idea. In fact, on November 12, 1984, the UN General Assembly adopted a Declaration on the Right of Peoples to Peace, which affirmed, "the peoples of our planet have a sacred right to peace." The declaration said that this right "constitutes a fundamental obligation of each state," and the exercise of this right demands "the elimination of the threat of war," particularly nuclear war. Although the vote was ninety-two in favour and none opposed, there were thirty-four abstentions, and the declaration, absent any strategy for implementation, went on the shelf. The wars in Iraq (the First Gulf War), Somalia, Yugoslavia, Rwanda, and elsewhere left a sense that the international community had taken a wrong turn after the end of the Cold War and was missing a golden opportunity to build a better foundation for peace.

In 1997, Federico Mayor, the Director-General of the United Nations Educational, Scientific and Cultural Organization (UNESCO), presented a new elaboration with two strategies: first, immediate action on urgent issues such as poverty, environmental destruction, and international justice through strengthening the UN system; and second, a massive education campaign focused on youth and designed to foster an understanding and tolerance of other cultures. The Norwegian Institute of Human Rights followed up with a new draft outlining peace as a human right, peace as a duty, and the development of peace through programs promoting a culture of peace. Through identifying the roots of global problems and addressing conflicts early, the right to peace came into better focus as a global ethic of non-violence and reverence for life.

A remarkable debate then took place at UNESCO's general conference in 1997. One European country after another either attacked or expressed reservations about the right to peace. Countries from the South struck back, accusing the North of wanting to protect their arms industries. Paraguay jabbed at the North: "Perhaps peace is a greater concern in the South where scarce resources are being diverted to war." Seeing that prospects for a consensus were hopeless, Mayor pulled back. During the next two years, the debate shifted to a somewhat less contentious topic, a culture of peace, which is not seen as a "right" but an "approach" that seeks to transform the cultural tendencies toward war and violence into a culture where dialogue, respect, and fairness govern social relations. In this way, violence can be prevented through a more tolerant common global ethic. Mayor formulated a Declaration and Programme of Action on a Culture of Peace, and rounds of debate at UNESCO followed. At one point, the US delegate, probably unwittingly, put his finger precisely on why a human right to peace is needed: "Peace should not be elevated to the category of a human right, otherwise, it will be very difficult to start a war."

While certainly more digestible than the right to peace, a culture of peace should not be seen as an anodyne substitute. For, if society became less bellicose and more supportive of even elementary social justice in a world of intense competition over resources, recourse to war would decline as the years pass. Codifying the right to peace might then be more easily obtained.

WAR IS A PRODUCT OF CULTURE

A culture of peace is not just a collection of amorphous paeans to harmony on a good day. It is rooted in a new understanding that human beings are not genetically programmed for war. There is no inherent biological component of our nature that produces violence. This was the conclusion of the Seville Statement on Violence drafted in 1986 by twenty leading biological and social scientists under the auspices of the International Society for Research on Aggression. After examining arguments based on evolution, genetics, animal behaviour, brain research, and social psychology, the scientists drew the conclusion that biology does not predestine us to war and violence. "We conclude that biology does not condemn humanity to war, and that humanity can be freed from the bondage of biological pessimism." War, the scientists said, is a product of culture.

Throughout the twentieth century, wars were the first choice of most governments in dealing with conflict. It seemed "natural" to go to war against a perceived evil. But that does not mean that humanity cannot get out of the sociological trap of the culture of war. There is no denying the presence of evil in the world, which all too often manifests itself in violence. But war in response to violence is no longer the only option. The point here is that humanity has achieved a level of maturation where aggression can be controlled and dealt with by new mechanisms, such as the International Criminal Court and internationally sponsored peacekeeping operations. Humanity is slowly climbing out of the pitiless hole of warfare that has claimed so many lives. We now know that it is possible to put war behind us, even if political practitioners are not yet ready to dismantle the war machinery.

Using the Seville Statement as a guide, UNESCO outlined a culture of peace embracing a set of ethical and aesthetic values, habits, customs, attitudes toward others, forms of behaviour, and ways of life that would reject violence and respect the life, dignity, and human rights of all individuals. In a culture of peace, the old images of the culture of war would give way to understanding, tolerance, and solidarity; democratic participation would replace authoritarian governance; sustainable economic and social development would replace exploitation of the weak and of the environment.

This work led to the UN General Assembly's adoption on September 13, 1999, of a Declaration and Programme of Action on a Culture of Peace, regarded at the time as the most comprehensive program for peace ever undertaken by the UN. It set out a route to ending violence through education, dialogue and cooperation, commitment to peaceful settlement of conflicts, promotion of the right to development, equal rights and opportunities for women and men, and freedom of expression, opinion, and information. A group of Nobel Peace Prize laureates drew up guidelines, which were translated into more than fifty languages: Respect all life; reject violence; share with others; listen to understand; preserve the planet; rediscover solidarity. Programs and petitions were organized by 180 international organizations around the world to mark the International Year for the Culture of Peace in 2000. An International Decade for a Culture of Peace and Non-Violence for the Children of the World was designated for 2001–2010. Then 9/11 struck.

Some analysts have written that the terrorist attacks on the World Trade Center and the Pentagon were the real opening of the twenty-first century and that the "war on terror" defines how we will live as the century progresses. I disagree. It is true that a sense of fear pervaded the general populace and security systems upended to head off future attacks. There will always be individuals willing to give their lives to attack an enemy. But terrorism is an aberration, not a system of change in people's lives and attitudes toward one another. There are no civil society groups by the thousands coalescing around terrorism; rather, there are civil society groups by the tens of thousands implementing at ground level, in one way or another, the values of a culture of peace. This huge and often unsung movement that rejects war provides a transformative moment for humanity. It is still overshadowed by the immense news coverage of intra-state wars and other forms of strife. The movement to a culture of peace, however "soft" it may appear on the surface compared to the "hard" decisions of warfare still lingering in the militarists' offices, is the real power of the twenty-first century. The momentum of history, buttressed by new life-enhancing technologies, is on the side of the culture of peace.

GROWING WILLINGNESS TO WORK FOR PEACE

When the UN held the culture of peace debates in the late 1990s, Mayor having retired from UNESCO, the chief promoter was Ambassador Anwarul Chowdhury of Bangladesh, who later became the UN's High Representative for Least Developed Countries, Landlocked Developing Countries and Small Island Developing States. The gregarious Chowdhury became one of the most popular and effective diplomats at the UN. At one point in his diplomatic career, he was president of the Security Council and used the position to prepare the way for the adoption of the groundbreaking UN Security Council resolution on the role of women in peace and security. For this work, he was awarded the Chancellor's Medal for Global Leadership for Peace by the University of Massachusetts at Boston. We greeted each other as friends when we sat down to talk in the Vienna Café in the UN Building. I asked him what accounts for his optimism, and his answer paralleled Carlos Villan Duran's assessment.

"I believe there is a critical mass of people throughout the world who want a genuine peace," he said, "a peace that is just and sustainable and that benefits everybody. And it is women who have blossomed as community leaders in many countries, such as Sierra Leone, Mali, and Sri Lanka, who are making a real difference. Though conflicts and hatred have continued, there is a growing willingness to work for peace. That makes me hopeful."

"How badly was the culture of peace set back by 9/11 and the Iraq war?" I asked him. "Is it functioning sufficiently so that it is actually laying the basis for the right to peace?"

"Well, I believe 9/11 actually strengthened the urging for a culture of peace. Many people suddenly realized that nations don't have to go to war to cause human insecurity, and unless we strengthen the fabric of our society with the values of a culture of peace and the right to peace, we cannot survive. The right to peace is stuck, so to speak, in the inter-governmental context, but the overwhelming opinion of people around the world now supports the idea of the right to peace."

He added: "I strongly believe that the flourishing of a culture of peace will generate the mindset that is an essential prerequisite for humanity's transition from force to reason, from conflict and violence to dialogue and peace." The very fact that governments are working on the draft declaration is a remarkable step forward, he said. But he is uneasy that powerful governments, unwilling to let go of the "hardware" approach to peace, are still denying a consensus on the concept of the right to peace.

When the UN Human Rights Council set in motion the formal study of the draft Declaration on the Right to Peace, the vote was thirty-four in favour, one against, and twelve abstentions. The US took a stand at the outset that it opposed the concept of the right to peace, let alone what the draft declaration contained. Nonetheless, it joined eighty other states at an inter-governmental working group meeting in Geneva in February 2013 to examine the draft text. It was here that the divisions over peace burst out into the open.

THE CONTROVERSIAL AGENDA FOR PEACE

The draft text begins with a preamble "reaffirming the common will of all people to live in peace with one another" and expressing a conviction that the prohibition of the use of force is the primary international prerequisite for the well-being of countries and for the full implementation of human rights and fundamental freedoms. It expresses "the will of all peoples that the use of force must be eradicated from the world, including through full nuclear disarmament, without delay." Its fourteen articles start off by proclaiming a principle: "Individuals and peoples have a right to peace ... The right to peace is related to all human beings, including civil, political, economic, social, and cultural rights." It moves into controversial terrain when it states that mechanisms should be developed "to eliminate inequality, exclusion and poverty, as they generate structural violence, which is incompatible with peace." And then: "All peoples and individuals have the right to have the resources freed by disarmament allocated to the economic, social and cultural development of peoples and to the fair redistribution of natural wealth, responding especially to the needs of the poorest countries ..."

The draft proclaims conscientious objection to military service, regulates private military and security companies, and
protects migrants. "Everyone shall enjoy . . . the right to adequate
food, drinking water, sanitation, housing, health care, clothing, education, social security and culture." The environment is
included: "Everyone has the right to a safe, clean and peaceful
environment, including an atmosphere that is free from dangerous man-made interference . . ."

At the very least, the draft shows how complex the subject of
peace is. If peace is to include every social benefit imaginable,
and then to make that a right, it is not likely that such a universal
state of satisfaction can be obtained. And yet, as has been said
many times, there can be no peace without the development
of peoples. The problem with the declaration is that it seeks to
codify what many think should remain a goal or an aspiration.
Thus well-trained international lawyers diligently pursue the
legalities underlying every phrase. Is the right to peace an individual or collective right? Lawyers incessantly debate this point.

At the outset of the inter-governmental meeting, the US
made its opposition clear: "We do not recognize the existence of
a 'right' to peace." The US position is that, although the country
is deeply concerned whenever conflict erupts and human rights
are violated, the foundational documents of the UN have never
defined peace as a right, rather a goal to be achieved through
the full implementation of human rights, and that by drawing
into the draft declaration a range of issues still being debated in
UN forums and making them rights, the process confuses and
endangers harmonious international progress. Canada joined
the US objections: "Canada does not accept that a stand-alone
'right to peace' exists under international law. As such we do not
see the justification for negotiating a declaration on this concept. Peace is not a human right in and of itself. It is rather a goal
that can be best realized through the enforcement of existing

identifiable and distinguishable human rights."

With attitudes so hard at the outset, the road to agreement on a declaration, even if shorn of its most controversial points, will be a rocky one. But that is what the exercise of diplomacy is for. Duran wants to build on the existing consensus that human rights, peace, and development are interdependent and mutually reinforcing and that any efforts to solidify the peace process should be guided by the UN Charter in addition to a vast jurisprudence inspired by international law. In applying the Charter, however, the problems mount. Article 2(4) of the Charter says: "All Members shall refrain in their international relations from the threat or use of force against the territorial integrity or political independence of any state. . ." The opponents of codifying peace say that's enough to ensure a peaceful atmosphere. But of course it isn't, because it does not constrain corrupt regimes from warring on their own people.

The proponents of a right to peace further argue that the flagrant misuse of Article 51 is an additional reason for codifying a right to peace. Article 51 says: "Nothing in the present Charter shall impair the inherent right of individual or collective self-defence if an armed attack occurs against a Member of the United Nations, until the Security Council has taken measures necessary to maintain international peace and security . . ." The US used Article 51 in its pre-emptive attack on Iraq, claiming that it was acting in self-defence against Iraq's suspected weapons of mass destruction (a suspicion later proved fallacious). So it seems that, just as the Charter is deficient in not banning nuclear weapons (which were not invented when the Charter was written), the Charter by itself cannot fully resolve the claimed inherent right to peace.

FINDING THE RIGHT SPEED OF ACTION

A favourable resolution may be obtained by putting greater reliance on Article 28 of the Universal Declaration of Human Rights:

"Everyone is entitled to a social and international order in which the rights and freedoms set forth in this Declaration can be fully realized." When this article is viewed in the context of the values of non-violence contained in the culture of peace documents, a more positive environment for discourse is produced. The debate can then build on the agreement already reached by world leaders who, at the 2005 summit marking the sixtieth anniversary of the UN, said, "We . . . reaffirm our commitment to work towards a security consensus based on the recognition that many threats are interlinked, that development, peace, security and humans rights are mutually reinforcing . . . and that all states need an effective and efficient collective security system pursuant to the purposes and principles of the Charter."

The proponents of a right to peace, however, don't want generalities; at least they want the declaration, in the forum of the Human Rights Council, to pronounce on specifics, such as the immediate elimination of nuclear weapons. But these specific demands are still being debated in a range of other forums. By trying to codify the right to peace at a very early stage in the budding culture of peace, the proponents run the risk of deepening divisions in the international community. Still, they are not wrong to press their case now. The strategy of timing is a judgment call. If people who want peace — a defined peace — do not speak up, the militarists will continue to dominate the public debates. We must find the right course and speed of action to balance the urgent need for the world community to come together in a common understanding of what needs to be done to achieve peace with the orderly construction of the legal mechanisms to guarantee it.

Duran insists that it is urgent to "to clarify the legal content of the emerging human right to peace" and that the Human Rights Council "has the competence to deal with the codification and progressive development of the human right to peace."

Unfortunately, that is a very disputable notion, given that the Human Rights Council, whose forty-seven seats of three-year terms are obtained by election within the UN system, does not enjoy a salubrious reputation. It is frequently criticized for allowing countries with poor human rights records to be members and for being preoccupied with the Arab-Israeli conflict.

When the council returned to the issue at its meeting in June 2013, the US stiffened its opposition to negotiating a text on the right to peace. This time it was joined by the European Union. But the opponents have left the door open for some progress at future meetings if the subject became a "discussion on the linkage between peace and the enjoyment of human rights." Christian Guillermet, a Costa Rican diplomat who heads the UN committee working on the draft declaration, has seized on the possibilities of a new text, softening the language in an effort to find a consensus for general acceptance. The choice of a representative of Costa Rica, a country without an army, to lead the process seems inspired.

I interviewed Ambassador Guillermet, who calls himself a "passionate diplomat," by Skype in Geneva just before he set out on a lengthy journey to many countries to test the waters for common agreement on a more moderate declaration. "I want to use transparency, inclusiveness, consensus, and objectivity in presenting a new text," he said. "I'm asking everybody to be flexible so that we can find a consensus. Even those who are most sceptical may be brought around by this approach. I am optimistic that we can establish the relationship between human rights and peace."

"A uniting of views will require good faith on all sides," I said. "I hope that those countries who said they were open to continued discussion will maintain good faith in recognizing that you are moving in their direction. But they can't hold up the process in which the international community wants to avert war." "I have to show good faith myself," he responded. "All states must realize that I am being transparent. Do we insist on the right to peace or manage the idea by taking a small step forward? The 'right to peace' needs education and improved international relations before it can be enunciated clearly. My personal view is that we need to move forward a little bit and negotiate the title at the end."

At this moment in history, most nations are ready to listen to the moral call for peace as distinct from dealing with the legal imperatives of a dozen disputed components put together in one declaration. A simplified declaration, one based on a moral call, would stand a better chance of wide acceptance. It would be more productive to highlight the political value of a simple declaration than to hold out for a declaration with a supposed legal base. Even a more general non-binding declaration of the right to peace might well act as a catalyst in spurring the peace agenda. The Universal Declaration of Human Rights, though only a non-binding document at the beginning, gave birth to a range of covenants and treaties enlarging the implementation of human rights in many aspects as the years went by. Over-reaching at the beginning jeopardizes long-range gains.

Would it not be enough to say that the right to peace is the right to pursue the benefits imparted by the Universal Declaration of Human Rights and subsequent legal instruments unimpeded by physical acts of warfare? That might not satisfy the most ardent proponents of the right to peace, but at least it would be a less contentious starting point and might hold the international community together. It would shift the focus to the fulfillment of peace through stopping warfare. As a politician and activist, I am concerned with building public opinion for the right to peace. I am not dismissing the fine points of law needed in any international agreement. But we stand a better chance of working out the law on the right to peace when the culture of peace plays a stronger role in our daily life.

The UN gives us the basis of international law to resolve human conflict even if peace is not yet legally defined. We may not have reached sufficient maturity of civilization to enforce the right to peace. Governments, at least some of them, are still too strong and are able to overcome the wishes of those who have turned against war. But this situation will not prevail forever. It will give way to those who demand the right to peace, just as the forces of slavery, colonialism, and apartheid gave way when the opposition became strong enough. That is why developing the elements of a culture of peace — education, sustainable development, respect for all human rights, equality between men and women, democratic participation, understanding and tolerance, free flow of information, and human security for all — is so important.

A culture of peace will not only make the world a more humane place, it will inexorably lead to the acquisition of the right to peace. A system of global governance for the common good of humanity must be our goal. Future generations, when they have tasted the fruit of a culture of peace, will recognize almost intuitively that peace is their right. They will demand it. Our role, in setting the twenty-first-century agenda, is to nourish the seeds of peace so that the blossom appears.

CHAPTER 6:
Promoting a Common Global Ethic

It was an ironic twist of timing that on the day I interviewed Nassir Abdulaziz Al-Nasser — head of the Alliance of Civilizations, which is dedicated to improving relations between Muslims and the West — news broke of the beheading of a British soldier on a London street by two young Muslim extremists. "I turned on the TV this morning and it reported the hacking of the young soldier by two bad guys who had no reason to do this," he said. "This is the kind of random act that worries me." In a moment, the grisly murder was flashed around the world, reinforcing the stereotype of Islamic terrorism; yet the work of the Alliance of Civilizations, in mobilizing action to improve cross-cultural understanding among countries and peoples, goes largely unheralded.

"The Alliance is a soft-power tool to prevent conflict and ease tensions by fostering dialogue among cultures and religions around the world," Al-Nasser told me. "The leadership of cultures and societies are moving to greater respect for one another, but isolated events of carnage undermine our work." He also expressed his chagrin at the Boston Marathon attack, which had occurred a few days earlier, and the rape of a young girl in Myanmar by two Buddhist soldiers. "Violence and intolerance can break out anywhere, and we need to build bridges everywhere," he said. "The important reality of our dialogue is not that we have differences in our religious and spiritual beliefs or practices, but how much we share in common. However the external trappings may differ, the quest for connection with a higher spiritual reality is common to us all. And the need for social harmony in the world is greater today than ever before."

Al-Nasser was Qatar's Ambassador to the UN for thirteen years before becoming president of the General Assembly in 2011. His term as president of the Security Council in 2006 was marked by the action he took to increase international co-operation to combat terrorism and to protect journalists in armed conflict. We spoke in the alliance's tiny offices tucked away in the Chrysler Building on Lexington Avenue, several blocks from UN headquarters in New York. Since, at age sixty, he would still presumably have several years of formal diplomacy ahead, I asked him why he had switched to the alliance from the heady positions he was used to. Speaking softly in measured tones, he described himself as "a Muslim, an Arab, and a diplomat who has lived most of my life in the West, and I have learned respect and co-operation. I loved multilateral work at the UN, with its wide range of networks. I thought that, with my friendly relations with member states and their permanent representatives, I could use this good investment to serve humanity for the sake of global stability. I believe the West and East, the North and South have a great potential for fostering mutual development through respect and co-operation."

The Alliance of Civilizations is an instructive example of how attitudes and human relationships are starting to influence international affairs to turn away from war and its handmaidens, revenge and retaliation. Religion plays an important role in developing a culture of peace, but the values of tolerance, respect, and reconciliation are also emerging from secular endeavours to

build the conditions for peace, and the alliance is in the forefront
of these efforts.

AN ALLIANCE, NOT CLASH, OF CIVILIZATIONS

After young Muslim terrorists attacked trains in Madrid on
March 11, 2004, killing 191 people and injuring two thousand,
Spanish Prime Minister Rodriguez Zapatero proposed in the UN
General Assembly that an "alliance of civilizations" project be created as an international response to the terrorist attacks. Rather
than reacting provocatively as occurred after 9/11, Zapatero
pleaded with the international community to prevent hatred and
incomprehension from building a wall between the Western and
the Arab and Muslim worlds. Such a wall would certainly produce a "clash of civilizations," he warned. In contrast, an alliance
of civilizations would reaffirm the increasing interdependence of
all societies in the areas of economics, finance, security, culture,
environment, and health. The central aim of the alliance would be
to strengthen diversity so it becomes a source of enrichment and
not a threat. The Turkish government, with its eye constantly on
both Europe and the Islamic world, was also interested in the idea
of promoting harmony among cultures and civilizations. Turkish Prime Minister Recep Tayyip Erdogan joined Zapatero in
co-sponsoring the alliance initiative. UN Secretary-General Kofi
Annan established a high-level group to probe the issue. Federico
Mayor, who had become president of the Culture of Peace Foundation in Spain, and Professor Mehmet Aydin, theologian and
Turkish Minister of State, were named co-chairs. Other notable
members included former president Seyed Mohamed Khatanu of
Iran, Nobel laureate Archbishop Desmond Tutu of South Africa,
and the religious historian Karen Armstrong.

The high-level group's report dealt immediately with religious extremism, where fundamentalist and extremist ideologies
have been used to justify acts of violence and terrorist attacks

on civilians. The report emphasized that none of the world's religions condone or approve the killing of innocents. All religions promote the ideals of compassion, justice, and respect for the dignity of human life. "Recently, a considerable number of acts of violence and terrorism have been committed by radical groups on the fringes of Muslim societies. Because of these actions, Islam is perceived by some as an inherently violent religion. Assertions to this effect are manifestly incorrect and at worst maliciously motivated. They deepen divides and reinforce the dangerous mutual animosity among societies." The report pointed out that no single group or culture had a monopoly on extremism and terrorist acts in the twentieth century. In fact, secular political motives were responsible for some of the most horrifying reigns of terror in living memory, such as the Holocaust, the Stalinist repressions in the Soviet Union, and more recent genocides in Cambodia, the Balkans, and Rwanda, all perpetrated by state powers.

The group found that the rise in modern hostility between Western and Muslim societies lies not in the ancient past but in developments in the last two centuries, starting with European imperialism and the resulting emergence of anti-colonial movements. The tortuous Palestinian-Israeli conflict, Western prosperity built on Middle East oil, and Western and Muslim accusations of double standards have all exacerbated tensions, and all of this worsened by media coverage that gives time and space mostly to the most extreme of the religious voices in the Muslim world and to the most anti-Muslim ideologues in the West. They made a number of practical suggestions for ending the prolonged Palestinian-Israeli conflict, the violence in Afghanistan, and the war in Iraq. But the long-range value of the report lay in its suggestions to overcome the mutual fear, suspicion, and ignorance across cultures that have spread beyond political leaders into the hearts and minds of populations. The report called for action in four areas: education, youth, migration, and media programs to reduce cross-cultural tensions and build bridges between communities.

DEVELOPING VOICES OF MODERATION

In one of his last acts before stepping down as Secretary-General, Annan accepted the report and established a small Alliance of Civilizations office at the UN. The alliance began with sponsoring local and regional programs in the Middle East, Southern Europe, Africa, Central Asia, and North America in the four designated fields highlighted in the report. It has trained hundreds of journalists in different regions around the world on how to report on culturally divisive issues, and teamed up with Google and the Jordan Media Institute to provide a platform for young journalists in the Middle East to share cross-cultural insights and experiences. When zealots released an anti-Islam video on YouTube in 2012, the alliance launched a social media initiative to ensure that vocal and violent minorities did not drown out the voices of moderation. Through its fellowship program, students from North America and Europe travel to the Middle East and their counter-parts from the Middle East are brought to Europe and North America. A Youth Solidarity Fund provides funding for youth-led initiatives in two-dozen countries from Bangladesh to Tanzania.

A Global Forum has been held each year. I attended the first of these, in Madrid in 2008, where one thousand political, religious, corporate, and civil society leaders conducted stimulating dialogues on reducing polarization between nations and launched joint initiatives to promote cross-cultural understanding globally. By the time of the fifth forum, attended by 2,500, the alliance had become, as Al-Nasser said, "a really global undertaking, with universal aims and raising awareness of the urgent need to promote responsible leadership in all fields of action." Shortly after, an inter-governmental meeting of Friends of the Alliance of Civilization was held at the UN, attended by the representatives of 115 countries and twenty-three international organizations. "The theory of a 'clash of civilizations' is not convincing," the Spanish delegate told the gathering, "More and more people want to join in our work to shape the world and live in coexistence and peace. We must know each other better, respecting our differences."

Operating in the framework of tension-filled Muslim-Western relations, the alliance has, not surprisingly, drawn criticism from those who perceive Islam as a permanent enemy of Western culture. Right-wing critics have charged that the goal of the alliance, even if not stated explicitly, is to impose the will of the UN on all Western countries. They claim that the alliance's secret agenda is to obtain for Islam a permanent seat on the Security Council and further undermine Israel. At the least, these critics see the alliance as a front for imposing a Palestinian government on the Middle East crisis. The UN Secretary-General has several times defended the alliance as necessary in galvanizing people to work on shared challenges of tolerance and respect and "to speak out against extremism and bigotry of any sort, including anti-Semitism and Islamophobia."

Al-Nasser recognizes the limitations, if not the dangers, of allowing the alliance to be characterized as dealing only with Muslim-Western relations. "The mission of the alliance is not just between the Muslim world and the West," he told me. "Maybe it was at the start, but we see many cultural and religious problems, not just between Muslims, Christians or Jewish. That's why we're now engaging in many regions, organizing seminars and workshops in many places and broadening our work to include the arts and sports. The Alliance is committed to promoting cooperative relations among diverse nations, peoples and cultures, and to diminishing tensions across civilizations."

Al-Nasser made the right move, for inter-religious conflict in today's world cuts across a wide swath of regions and cultures. The US State Department's highly detailed International Religious Freedom Report for 2012 recounts violence, restrictions, and abuse against several religions. While many nations uphold and protect religious freedom, other states subject members of religious minorities to violence, actively restrict citizens' religious freedom through oppressive laws and regulations, and fail to hold accountable those who attack fellow citizens out of religious hatred. In Nigeria, extremists in the Boko Haram sect have murdered hundreds of Christians and Muslims. Christians face constant danger in Afghanistan, Saudi Arabia, Somalia, and Iran. Christians have been killed even in several overwhelmingly Catholic nations, such as Colombia, Mexico, Burundi, South Sudan, and the Philippines. Anti-Semitic attacks in Egypt, Iran, Russia, and Argentina are commonplace. Also, it must not be forgotten that the most numerous victims of Muslim extremism are, in fact, other Muslims.

THE ARRIVAL OF PLURALISM

There is much human healing needed in the world. Fortunately, the climate for this work is becoming more propitious. Since the beginning of history, human beings have been at war with one another, often under the pretext of religion, ideology, or ethnicity. The Crusades — the series of Holy Wars between the eleventh and sixteenth centuries by the Christian states of Europe largely against Muslims but also against pagans, heretics, and people excommunicated for political, economic, and religious reasons — are a distasteful memory. Today, we are confronted with international terrorism, which misuses religious ideas for perverse ideological purposes and kills innocent people indiscriminately. Terrorism, however, does not dominate the world agenda. Violence and terror have certainly not disappeared, but, compared to earlier centuries and even the first half of the twentieth century, when I grew up, they are greatly reduced. The growth of tolerance and acceptance, brought about by the Universal Declaration of Human Rights, is a big factor in the reduction of violent conflict, and it has laid the groundwork for modern efforts such as the Alliance of Civilizations to take hold.

The hallmark of our time is not the ethno-centralism so dominant in the past, but the arrival of pluralism. As former UN Secretary-General Kofi Annan put it: "I see the world coming together in one global civilization, to which each of us brings our own traditions, cultures, and beliefs." Though fractures and suspicions are evident, the beginning of a global community, brought together by communications, transportation, trade, finance, and environmental challenges, has emerged. Diversity of peoples and cultures is now managed rather than left floundering as in the past. Religion plays a role in the harmonizing of peoples, and I will shortly discuss this, but here I want to note that supra-religious forces are largely responsible for modern efforts to end the old cultural antagonisms. The development of a "global conscience" transcending religious doctrines accounts for the progress made in building the conditions for a peaceful coexistence.

The first article of the Universal Declaration of Human Rights, adopted in 1948, says, "All human beings are born free and equal in dignity and rights." The preamble asserts that violations of human rights have "outraged the conscience of mankind." These seminal statements spawned covenants on the civil, political, economic, social, and religious rights of all peoples. Questions about the well-being of the citizens of the planet and of the planet itself are now the stuff of daily politics. Driven forward by science and technology and a new understanding of the inherency of human rights, humanity is becoming more integrated. Not only do we know one another across what used to be great divides, but we also know that we need one another for common survival. There is a new caring for the human condition and the state of the planet. This is the awakening of a global conscience. Neither the still-existing regional conflicts nor the personal greed that leads to conflict can deny, let alone overcome, the rising sense of a global ethic. This ethic of human rights and planetary steward-ship stems from the global conscience.

Such a development in human thinking — in which the world, not just our region, has become our neighbourhood — is unparalleled in history. Through the centuries, philosophers and prophets have called us to a higher manifestation of mor-ality and social justice. Such spiritual concepts stood virtually apart from the daily business of governments. In the past seven decades — the lifetime so far of the United Nations — these concepts have entered daily thinking through highly pragmatic political discourse. Although the term *social justice* is not usu-ally found in UN documents, much of the UN's activity is directed at repairing the injustices of poverty and the ravages of war. The Millennium Development Goals are an expression of social justice. We still suffer global forces promoting self-ishness, greed, and the raw exercise of power, but there is an opposite force composed of many like-minded governments and civil society and promoting the global values of tolerance, diversity, and pluralism along with fair-trade practices. Though the two forces often appear to be at a standoff, for the first time in history, great numbers of civil society are assembling to pres-sure the powerful to adopt equitable policies. When the leaders of the world assembled at the UN in 2005 to commemorate the organization's sixtieth anniversary, they issued a declaration showing how global conscience has taken hold. "In order to promote peace and security," they stated, "we commit ourselves to advancing human welfare, freedom and progress every-where, as well as to encouraging tolerance, respect, dialogue and cooperation among cultures, civilizations and peoples." Actually doing all this would require another step forward in political leadership. Nonetheless, global conscience is potent and its full development offers the greatest hope for peace in the history of humanity.

RELIGIONS FOR PEACE

Religious communities, the largest and best-organized civil institutions in the world and claiming the allegiance of billions of every race and culture, are best equipped to speak to and, in their best moments, reflect the rising global conscience. A central base for this work is 777 UN Plaza, a twelve-storey building on the corner of First Avenue and 44th Street, directly across from the United Nations headquarters in New York. Known as the Church Center, the building houses more than a dozen religious and community organizations working on the many UN agenda items. Ranging from the Methodist Division of World Peace to the World Council of Churches, these activists keep track of UN committee debates, lobby UN delegates on the margins of meetings, and report back to their congregations.

I visited the offices of Religions for Peace and spoke with Jude Nnorom, Conflict Transformation Officer, who was born in Eastern Nigeria in 1968, just as that country ended its civil war. An Ibo tribesman, Nnorom became a Catholic priest with a strong desire to help resolve the continuing clashes in Nigeria over oil and land. "I was attracted to interfaith work," he told me. "I wanted to use the spiritual and moral strength we find in Christianity and Islam to teach people non-violence." He obtained a Master's degree in peace studies at the University of Notre Dame in Indiana and came to Religions for Peace as an intern. He said he was looking forward to returning to Africa to work in the conflict resolution field.

I was first attracted to Religions for Peace in 1974 when I

attended the organization's world forum at Leuven, Belgium, and was exposed to the diversity of religions that make up the faith spectrum. It was there that I met Thich Nhat Hanh, the Vietnamese Buddhist monk and poet who became a famous Zen master and one of the leading peace figures in the world. His commitment to non-violence has inspired countless followers around the world. Drawing into its work leading religious activists, Religions for Peace has become the largest international coalition of representatives from the world's great religions dedicated to promoting peace. It is headed by William Vendley, an American theologian with a Ph.D. from Fordham University who pioneered religious co-operation as a tool to help resolve conflict. He helped start the Inter-religious Council of Bosnia-Herzegovina after the civil war, which led to a historic commitment of the religious communities to rebuild a single, multi-ethnic Bosnia. The organization did similar work in Sierra Leone, and convened senior Iraqi religious leaders in Amman shortly after the occupation of Iraq to start co-operating in the provision of humanitarian assistance.

In Ethiopia, Eritrea, Sierra Leone, Liberia, Indonesia, Sri Lanka, and several other countries, Religions for Peace has helped prevent conflicts, mediate peace among warring parties, and rebuild societies in the aftermath of violence. The organization holds that religious communities are called on not only to reject war, sectarian violence, weapons proliferation, and human rights abuses, but also to identify and confront the root causes of injustice, economic inequalities, governance failures, development obstacles, social exclusions, and environmental abuses.

MUSLIMS AND CHRISTIANS WORKING TOGETHER

Perhaps the most dramatic example of inter-religious co-operation in recent times is A Common Word. In 2007, 138 Muslim scholars wrote a public letter to Christian leaders affirming the common ground of love of God and love of neighbour that Muslims and Christians stand on. Some three hundred Christian leaders responded with enthusiasm. The organization A Common Word was formed and a series of interfaith meetings started. In its first five years, it became an influential dialogue forum, providing a common ground on which thousands of Muslim and Christian religious leaders have been brought together. It has contributed significantly to reducing tensions between these two communities who together comprise 55 per cent of the world's population. It sent a Muslim-Christian peace delegation to address inter-communal strife in Nigeria in 2012 and inspired a unanimous resolution at the UN General Assembly for adopting a World Interfaith Harmony Week to be celebrated annually in the first week of February. The Archbishop of Canterbury, Rowan Williams, convened a gathering of international religious leaders, including significant Muslim religious leaders, to identify shared values and ways to promote mutual understanding. Participants urged their faith communities to act compassionately towards all those affected by financial and environmental crises.

The driving figure behind A Common Word is Prince Ghazi bin Muhammad, the grandson of King Talal I and a prominent scholar in Jordan, who has held numerous education and religious posts. Prince Ghazi was educated at Princeton and Cambridge, and quickly established himself as a leading interpreter of Islam to the Western world. In an interview by Skype at his office in Amman, we discussed how A Common Word had achieved a breakthrough in scholarly dialogue between Muslim and Christian leaders enabling them to see the "genuine spirituality" of each other. He recognized that the organization must do more to have this new respect filter down to everyday life in the mosques and churches.

"This is part of the projection of a global conscience," I said. "How do you see A Common Word moving beyond scholarship to play a role in further diminishing violent conflict in the world?"

"All our initiatives cannot resolve conflict," he responded. "What we can do is show there is no theological ground for conflict. If a conflict is for political reasons, there must be a political solution with healing afterwards. The particular niche we have is to show that fighting is not based on a true interpretation of religion. Don't say you're fighting for God or that God wants you to fight. Say you're fighting over resources, say you're fighting for anything, but don't bring God into the reasons for fighting. That I think we can do effectively."

I pointed out that from their different starting points both the Alliance of Civilizations and A Common Word, as relatively new instruments for peace in the world, possess the power to influence many people to change their views of adherents of other cultures and religions, and perhaps they should work more closely together. "We have tried to support each other," he said, "but the structures and work of each, though complementary, are distinct. We need a few more years to get the work of each to trickle down to greater numbers."

"The protection of common ground and common values throughout the world is a challenge of the highest moral order," I observed. "We need both religion and secularism to raise our hopes for humanity."

He responded by pointing to the dangers posed by a new demagoguery facilitated by social media, the worsening environment, and resource scarcities. "I worry that these will set off another round of wars and conflicts twenty or thirty years from now. I hope religious leaders will use their teaching role to speak against the demagoguery that produces wars."

Prince Ghazi, concentrating on strengthening the relationship between today's Muslim and Christian leaders, welcomed Pope Benedict XVI when the pontiff visited a mosque in

Amman. For his part, Benedict received a delegation from A Common Word and sponsored workshops in the Vatican. A joint statement said that believers "are called to be instruments of love and harmony . . . renouncing oppression, aggressive violence and terrorism, especially that committed in the name of religion, and upholding the principle of justice for all."

The Pope's welcome went a long way towards ameliorating his earlier maladroit speech in which he quoted an unfavourable remark about Islam made by a fourteenth-century Byzantine emperor. Many Islamic politicians and religious leaders protested against what they saw as an insulting mischaracterization of Islam. The Pope apologized for the misunderstanding and in a later journey to the Middle East spoke of his "deep respect for the Muslim community." The official position of the Catholic Church toward Islam, as stated by the Second Vatican Council, is highly favourable. "Upon the Muslims . . . the Church looks with esteem," the council said. "Although in the course of centuries many quarrels and hostilities have arisen between Christians and Muslims, this most sacred Synod urges all to forget the past and to strive sincerely for mutual understanding. On behalf of all mankind, let them make common cause of safeguarding and fostering social justice, moral values, peace and freedom."

"PEACE ON EARTH": A PROBING DOCUMENT

Just as the four-year (1962–1965) Vatican Council was getting under way, a religious document appeared that reached out to all humanity in a probing call for peace that has seldom been equalled. It was a papal encyclical called "Peace on Earth," written by Pope John XXIII, a gregarious Italian prelate whose openness captured the attention of the world. He had played a role in the Cuban missile crisis of 1962, urging US President John F. Kennedy and Soviet leader Nikita Khrushchev to go into dialogue to end the most dangerous confrontation of the Cold War. His message to Moscow and Washington, begging the leaders not to remain deaf to the cry of humanity, appeared in newspapers around the world, including *Pravda*, the official newspaper of the Soviet Communist Party. Shortly after, Pope John brought out his encyclical in which he projected a world where peace would be achieved by governments implementing human rights and where global institutions would address humanity's needs.

Sentence after sentence struck at the heart of the human condition in the mid-twentieth century. People have "the right to live," he affirmed. They have "the right to bodily integrity . . . to food, clothing, shelter, medical care, rest and social services." It is not right that people live in constant fear of war and violence. "Nuclear weapons must be banned." "True and lasting peace among nations cannot consist in the possession of an equal supply of armaments but only in mutual trust." The United Nations must "adapt its structure and methods of operation to the magnitude and nobility of its tasks." He insisted that nations would find peace only through common security. "The attainment of the common good is the sole reason for the existence of civil authorities." His words foreshadowed the Vatican Council's major document, *The Constitution on the Church in the Modern World*, which elaborated on the joys and hopes, the grief and anxieties we all have irrespective of religion, race, or culture. As the years went by, Pope John's vision began to be realized: Human rights were extended, more international agencies created, crimes against humanity prosecuted, nuclear weapons reductions pursued. John XXIII never visited the United Nations, but his three successors did. Popes Paul VI, John Paul II, and Benedict XVI all came to the New York headquarters to give their full support to the UN's peace agenda. The Holy See maintains a permanent observer delegation at the UN, which makes statements on all the key issues. Pope Francis's deep concern, in the mode of John XXIII, for the poor of the world and the extension of human rights prompted the editors of *Time* magazine to select him as the 2013 "Person of the Year," barely nine months after his election. The world wants to hear more from a pope who expresses such outrage: "How can it be that it is not news when an elderly homeless person dies of exposure, but it is news when the stock market loses two points?" Already, his leitmotif has become: "The rich must help, respect and promote the poor."

In April 2013, on the fiftieth anniversary of the publication of "Peace on Earth," I spoke at a conference at the Catholic University of America in Washington, D.C., and recalled how John XXIII's words had inspired me to devote my public life to working for peace with social justice for all. A featured speaker at the conference was Cardinal Peter Turkson, who heads the Pontifical Commission for Justice and Peace, a Vatican body that was a direct offshoot of "Peace on Earth." Cardinal Turkson had just been in the news in the run-up to the conclave that elected Pope Francis because Turkson was himself considered a candidate to become the first "black pope." His background greatly appealed to the world press.

He was born in 1948, the fourth of ten children, in a two-room shack in Wassaw Nsuta, a village in Western Ghana. His Catholic father was a carpenter and his Methodist mother sold vegetables in the open market. He had a paternal uncle who was a Muslim. He did his seminary studies in New York and later at the prestigious Pontifical Biblical Institute in Rome. He was appointed Archbishop of Cape Coast in Ghana in 1992 and went on to serve as president of the national bishops' conference before being named a cardinal in 2003. In 2009, after serving as general secretary for a synod of African bishops held in Rome, Turkson was named president of Justice and Peace, which is dedicated to "action-oriented studies" for the international promotion of justice, peace, and human rights. He was sent by Pope Benedict

to mediate conflict in the Ivory Coast. One of his major themes
is the need to reform political and financial institutions so that
they operate with more fairness to the world's disadvantaged
peoples. An accomplished polyglot, Turkson speaks English,
Fante, French, Italian, German, and Hebrew. Affable and with
a lively sense of humour, the cardinal is seen across Africa as a
dynamic church leader, particularly for his call for a "true world
political authority" to regulate a globalized economy.

I interviewed him at the Catholic University conference just
after he had given a major address on the impact of "Peace on
Earth." "You have said that nations are a stumbling block to the
development of a public authority in the world," I said, "What do
you think can be done about this?"

"If one talks about rights and duties, we need to have a body
to ensure that the rights and duties are implemented," he said.
"Who ensures this? Is it government? Nations are always competing against each other. Envy and greed continue to motivate
modern diplomacy. The global common good needs a corres-
ponding global authority. This is the thinking that can lead us
forward."

"Is the UN capable of doing this?" I asked. "The UN can be
reformed," he said. "The Security Council is not sufficiently representative. If it were reformed by having more representation of
peoples around the world, it would make everyone's voice heard
and be in a stronger position to uphold the common good."

He said lack of trust is one of the biggest impediments to
building the conditions for peace. This is particularly evident in
the field of nuclear weapons. "I'm appealing for common sense
to deal with the threat of nuclear terrorism by totally discarding
nuclear weapons. Nations are trying to gain advantage through
nuclear weapons superiority. We don't trust one another enough.
But we can't go on like this. The path to justice does not lie in
superior nuclear weaponry."

COMMON SCRIPTURAL TEACHING

A leitmotif of Cardinal Turkson's messages is for all people of good will to be peacemakers, to cultivate dialogue, and bring civilizations together "to witness the love of God's children precisely by yearning for peace for the future generations." This core idea drives virtually every major religion's teaching on peace. The Torah, the Bible, and the Koran all teach the uniqueness of God, prescribe good and prohibit wrong, and exhort forgiveness, charity, and love of fellow humans. The best of religious teaching today recognizes that we live in a multi-religious, multicultural, and pluralistic world in which all people of good will must unite to fight misunderstanding and hatred. One would think that such teaching would be welcomed into the councils of public policy making. Unfortunately, the public view of religion is that it has often been full of antagonisms even when not outright responsible for conflicts. Religion is pushed to the sidelines in present public discourse. The systematic neglect of religious factors blinds policy makers to the contribution religion could make to the public arena.

Some evangelical and fundamentalist leaders, convinced that the sole purpose of religion is to be a vehicle between humankind and God, ignore the practical social responsibilities that flow from the command to love our neighbour as ourself. The excessive introspection of these religionists leads to religious myopia. Thus the full power of religion to be an uplifting force in driving the production of public policies that fund human development and reduce the expensive machinery of war is lost. From time to time, religious leaders do come together to plead that governments properly address the problems of poverty, hunger, and social vulnerability. Religions for Peace, the Vatican's Justice and Peace Commission, and the periodic Parliament of the World's Religions, which holds a global dialogue of faiths, all send messages calling for a global ethic that would embrace a culture of non-violence and respect for life. These voices need to be heard in a secular world.

Religions will not lose by joining enthusiastically with secular humanists in the promotion of a global ethic centering on the well-being of humanity. On the contrary, religions would gain by manifesting their deep concern for the application of their own social justice principles.

CHAPTER 7:
Women: So Much to Offer the Peace Process

When Leymah Gbowee stood before the splendidly attired cream of Norwegian society to give her speech on receipt of the 2011 Nobel Peace Prize, she did not spare them the rawness of her life in Liberia that had brought her to the world stage: "Women had become the 'toy of war' for over-drugged young militias. Sexual abuse and exploitation spared no woman; we were raped and abused regardless of our age, religious, or social status. A common scene daily was a mother watching her young one being forcibly recruited or her daughter being taken away as the wife of another drug-emboldened fighter."

Gbowee, a champion of women's rights, is a brilliant example of women who have overcome violence to lead peacebuilding processes. In 2003, she led a band of women, armed with nothing but their convictions, in protesting against the ravages of the Liberian civil war and the murderous rampages of the president, Charles Taylor. The movement spread to fifty communities across Liberia. "We worked daily confronting warlords, meeting with dictators, and refusing to be silenced in the face of AK-47s and RPGs. We walked when we had no transportation, we fasted when water was unaffordable, we held hands in the face of danger, we spoke truth to power when everyone else was being diplomatic, we stood under the rain and the sun with our children to tell the world the stories of the other side of the conflict. Our educational backgrounds, travel experiences, faiths, and social classes did not matter. We had a common agenda: peace for Liberia now." Gbowee showed that the time had come when, as she told the Nobel gathering, "mothers are no longer begging for peace, but demanding peace, justice, equality, and inclusion in decision making."

I interviewed her by phone in her office in Monrovia, Liberia, and asked her if women were becoming a political force in Africa. "The thing you must understand is that the biggest number of voters in most of the world are women," she said. "So why are many women not in positions of authority? Most of the time we focus on the difficulties of political campaigns instead of mobilizing around our common identity as women. But we women of Liberia mobilized ourselves as victims of war and the hope of peace, and that is how we got Ellen Johnson Sirleaf elected the first woman president in modern Africa."

The Nobel committee awarded the 2011 prize jointly to three women, Gbowee, Sirleaf, and Tawakkol Karman of Yemen. The citation recognized them "for their non-violent struggle for the safety of women and for women's rights to full participation in peace-building work." The award was a huge lift to women peacemakers, who toil in many places in patience and creative actions. Gbowee paid tribute to this sisterhood: Women of Zimbabwe Arise, who face arrest and torture but remain the voice of the suffering people of Zimbabwe; Women of the Congo, who have endured horrific sexual violence in the endless Congo conflict; Women of Acholi Land in Uganda, who remain advocates for peace and justice despite torture and rape by the Lord's Resistance Army; Women of Afghanistan, where women have been subjected to honour killings after rape. The prize has come at a time, she said, "when women are throwing down the walls of repressive traditions with the invincible power of non-violence. Women are using their broken bodies from hunger, poverty, desperation, and destitution to stare down the barrel of a gun."

"WOMEN, WAKE UP"

Leymah Gbowee was born in central Liberia in 1972. When civil war broke out, she was a teenager and young mother and was sexually abused. She took a course offered by UNICEF to become a social worker able to counsel people traumatized by war. Conditions worsened and she fled to Ghana, living as a refugee until she returned to Liberia and started working with the Trauma Healing and Reconciliation Program. This was the start of her life as a peace activist. She earned a university degree from Mother Patern College of Health and Sciences and joined the West Africa Network for Peacebuilding, where Thelma Ekiyor of Nigeria, a lawyer who specialized in alternative dispute resolution, mentored her. Ekiyor brought Gbowee to the opening meeting of a women's offshoot of the Peacebuilding Network; the group of women from West African countries defined their work not just as anti-war activism but also as the elimination of structural forms of violence in everyday life, particularly systematic violence against women, such as rape, forced prostitution, and mutilation. Gbowee's courage grew and she was able to tell the painful parts of her story to the other women.

She took over the leadership of the women's network in Liberia and gathered a coterie of Christian and Muslim women to spread flyers at mosques and churches after prayers and at the Saturday market. The flyers read: "We are tired! We are tired of our children being killed! We are tired of being raped! Women, wake up — you have a voice in the peace process!" The movement grew to thousands of Liberian Muslim and Christian women praying for peace, and this led to daily non-violent demonstrations and sit-ins in defiance of the tyrannical president, Charles Taylor. The women went on a sex strike, a strategy inspired by the Greek play *Lysistrata* in which women withhold sex from their husbands to secure peace and end the Peloponnesian War. Gbowee says the strategy may or may not have been effective, but it garnered media attention to the movement.

The women, dressed in white, began daily sit-ins in a soccer field beside a highway used by Taylor each day. Taylor finally granted the women a hearing, and two thousand gathered outside his executive mansion while Gbowee went inside to make their case. She extracted a promise from the president to attend peace talks in Ghana with the Liberian rebel forces. When the negotiations stalled, Gbowee mounted another demonstration in Ghana, and this time the women threatened to disrobe unless a peace agreement was reached. "In Africa," she wrote in her memoirs, "it's a terrible curse to see a married or elderly woman deliberately bare herself." The tactic worked, and fourteen years of warfare in Liberia ended.

The United States Institute of Peace reported that the work of women all over Liberia was responsible for moving the peace process forward. Taylor went into exile in Nigeria, but his past caught up with him when the newly elected Sirleaf pressed charges against him. In 2012, in a special international tribunal in The Hague, Taylor was convicted of terror, murder, and rape and sentenced to fifty years in prison. The presiding judge said, "The accused has been found responsible for aiding and abetting as well as planning some of the most heinous and brutal crimes recorded in human history."

Gbowee wrote about the fragility of the peace the women had won: two hundred fifty thousand people dead, a quarter of them children; one in three persons displaced; one million people, mostly women and children, at risk of malnutrition, diarrhea, measles, and cholera because of contamination in wells; and 75 per cent of the country's roads, hospitals and schools destroyed. Worst was the trauma of the country. "A whole generation of young men had no idea who they were without a gun in their hands. Several generations of women were widowed, had been raped, seen their daughters and mothers raped, and their children kill and be killed. Neighbors had turned against neighbors; young people had lost hope, and old people, everything they had painstakingly earned. To a person, we were traumatized."

As the face of the peace movement in Africa, Gbowee continued to lead the women's network. But in 2004, frustrated at what she termed the cultural insensitivity of UN agencies imposing peace programs rather than working from the grassroots up, she began graduate studies at Eastern Mennonite University, a Christian college in Virginia specializing in conflict transformation and peacebuilding. International travel, greater influence at home, and fame followed, especially after a TV documentary, *Pray the Devil Back to Hell*, featuring the work of the African women culminating in the election of Sirleaf, was shown on the Internet.

THE TALENT FOR PEACEBUILDING

One of Gbowee's favourite themes is "unlocking the intelligence of women." I asked her to evaluate how women can play a greater role in peace and development issues. "Everyone possesses some intelligence, enabling them to move forward. Women especially know how to be peacemakers. They have the talent for peacebuilding and community building. When space is created for them to be safe and work without threat of oppression and violence, the skills come out. When the right environment is created, we can help them unlock their passion and intelligence and actions for the joy of peace." This "unlocking" is taking place in many areas, she said, pointing to the Democratic Republic of Congo, Ivory Coast, Egypt, Palestine, and Israel.

Gbowee, who has six children, has had many painful moments

in her life, and she says her Christian faith, learned from her mother who took her to a Lutheran church, has fortified her. Then she read a book, *The Politics of Jesus*, by John Howard Yoder, "which helped me put my Christian faith into the context of the social justice issues around me. Yoder's book, which has become a Christian classic, reveals how Jesus was always conscious of the agenda of politics and deeply concerned with social, political, and moral issues. "I asked myself, how can I be a Christian if I don't speak the truth? God has always helped me, especially at times when I wanted to give up."

Gbowee's story highlights two dimensions of women's involvement in war and peace issues. First, the violence committed against them is astounding. Violence against women is a global problem. As the Canadian author Sally Armstrong puts it in her book *Ascent of Women*, "Rape continues to be the ugly foundation of women's story of change . . . Today the taboo around talking about sexual violence has been breached. Women from Bosnia, Rwanda and the Democratic Republic of the Congo have blown the whistle about rape camps and mass rapes and even re-rape . . ."

Even though the International Criminal Court has declared rape a war crime, women are still far more likely than men to be subject to sexual violence in conflict zones. Neither national governments nor the international community has yet recognized the full extent of sexual violence as a major obstacle to women's engagement in the peace process. But the second lesson from Gbowee is that women are overcoming the violence done to them and should not be stereotyped as helpless victims of violence when, in fact, they have so much to offer the peace process. Fortunately, violence against women and gender discrimination are in decline (though too slowly), and because of the "ascent of women," to use Sally Armstrong's term, the long-term prospects for peace are brightening.

THE EFFECT OF EDUCATING WOMEN

I first noticed this in 1993 when the Canadian International Development Agency asked me to return to Bangladesh to retrace my trip of seventeen years earlier to see what had happened to the lives of people helped by Canadian aid projects. As I did the first time, I found the problems of Bangladesh, where recurrent floods, cyclones, and tidal waves constantly impede the development process, to be overwhelming. Yet I found Bangladesh to be moving ahead, largely because of the education of women and their increasingly strong role in the life of the country. Women by the hundreds of thousands were completing not only grade school but high school and going on to jobs in government and industry. They started going into politics. By 2013 there were one hundred women in the 350-seat parliament and the prime minister, leader of the opposition, and speaker were all women. The Bangladesh Alliance for Women Leadership trains women politicians and budding public service employees and teaches leadership and conflict resolution skills to women from a wide range of professional backgrounds. It is not an accident that the Bangladeshi parliament has become outspoken in its call for the full implementation of human rights and the elimination of nuclear weapons.

The ability of women to play a larger role in both national and international politics swells as the base of healthy, educated women grows. The base is becoming stronger thanks to the benefits women and girls are receiving from the Millennium Development Goals. Maternal deaths have been cut by nearly half since 1990. Gender parity in primary education has been achieved. The proportion of people without access to safe drinking water has been cut in half, with wide-ranging benefits for many, including women and girls who no longer need to spend their days collecting water in unsafe conditions and now have clean water to fight disease and infection. In too many countries, women are still being left behind. For example, two-thirds of the world's illiterate people are women. But the strengthening of women world-wide is shown in the impressive numbers of them succeeding in the professions and political endeavours.

The rising status of women burst onto the international stage with the 1995 Beijing Conference on Women: Action for Equality, Development and Peace, where 5,000 representatives from 189 governments and 2,100 non-governmental organizations adopted a wide-ranging platform of action to advance the interests of women. It amounted to a global commitment to achieving equality, development, and peace for women world-wide. In 2000, the UN Security Council followed up by adopting Resolution 1325, a groundbreaking measure on women, peace, and security because it was the first resolution to address the disproportionate and unique impact of armed conflict on women. It stressed the importance of women's equal and full participation as active agents in the prevention and resolution of conflicts, peacebuilding, and peacekeeping. Subsequent resolutions called for indicators to measure progress and made sexual violence in conflict a war crime, demanding that parties to armed conflict take appropriate measures to protect civilians from sexual violence, including training troops and enforcing disciplinary measures. This momentum spilled over to the creation in 2010 of UN Women, a department staffed by two thousand employees around the world, which focuses on gender equality and the empowerment of women. It operates on the principle that not only is gender equality a basic human right, but also that empowering women fuels economies, spurring productivity and growth.

I went to see the chief of the Peace and Security Section, Anne Marie Goetz, in UN Women's New York headquarters, located in the old Daily News Building on 42nd Street. Goetz, a former professor of political science at the Institute of Development

Studies, University of Sussex, had produced a huge binder of material identifying women's peace and security priorities and has made it available on a flash drive. There's no shortage of women around the world doing wonderful things to build peace, she told me, pointing to the list of one thousand women who had been collectively nominated in 2005 for the Nobel Peace Prize for their daily commitment to improving the lives of present and future generations. However, she added, "women continue to be poorly represented in formal peace processes, even though they contribute in many informal ways to conflict resolution." She said fewer than 8 per cent of participants in recent peace processes were women. "This exclusion invariably leads to a failure to adequately address women's concerns, such as sexual and gender-based violence, women's rights, and post-conflict accountability. When engaging major actors in a conflict in negotiation and resolution efforts, it is essential to involve women because their different experiences give them different perspectives on the social and economic ills to be addressed in any peace accord." Or as Leymah Gbowee puts it more bluntly, "Rape and abuse is the result of a larger problem, which is the absence of women in the decision-making space."

UN Women's work in peace and security is largely driven by Resolution 1325, which recognizes that conflict affects women and girls differently from men and boys, and that women must be part of conflict resolution and long-term peacebuilding. "For this to happen," Goetz has written, "a great deal needs to change in conflict prevention and resolution, peacekeeping and peacebuilding. And indeed much has changed. The protection of women and girls from sexual and gender-based violence is recognized to be a priority challenge for the humanitarian and peacekeeping practice. Women's coalition groups have grown in strength and are in some contexts able to put women's concerns on the agenda of peace talks." Nevertheless, she adds, there is still some distance to go to meet the expectations raised by the resolution.

Barriers include women's exclusion from peace processes, the absence or inadequate arrangements for women's security in refugee camps, low rates of indictments and convictions for war crimes against women, high levels of sexual violence in conflict, gender-based violence even after a conflict is over, and weak provisions for women's livelihood recovery needs. Goetz wants to see better security mechanisms for women, including in peacekeeping missions, and a rapid-response task team of judicial experts to support domestic transitional processes and to prevent impunity for these crimes. "A security and political response also means that peace negotiators and mediators must include sexual violence on peace talk agendas."

Where women have participated in peace talks, the results have been remarkable. In El Salvador in the 1990s, women were present at nearly all the negotiating tables, resulting in women being one-third of the beneficiaries of land redistribution and reintegration packages. In South Africa, the presence of women in the Multi-Party Negotiating Process acted as a catalyst for three million women participating in public discussions. In Northern Ireland, women secured a place at the peace table, built bridges between Catholics and Protestants, and promoted reconciliation and reintegration of political prisoners. But in the fourteen mediation processes the UN supported in 2011, representation of women among the negotiating parties was low, resulting in less attention being paid to the need to mobilize social movements for peace and build social reconciliation. Simply put, men generally still do not sufficiently value the inherently human approach women bring to conflict. It is true that some women have become combatants themselves, but most women are disposed to end conflict in a reconciliatory manner that advances gender equality and protects women's rights.

HOLDING OUT FOR GENDER EQUALITY

Goetz pointed to Luz Mendez, a delegate of the Guatemalan National Revolutionary Unity Party during the Guatemala peace talks in the mid-1990s, as an inspirational leader. Up to two hundred thousand people died or went missing during the thirty-six-year civil war in Guatemala, including about fifty thousand people who were "disappeared," mostly on orders of the government. In 2009, Guatemalan courts sentenced Felipe Cusanero as the first person convicted of the crime of ordering forced disappearances. In 2013 the former dictator Efraín Ríos Montt was found guilty of genocide for the killing of more than seventeen hundred indigenous Mayans during his 1982–1983 rule. He was the first former head of state to be tried for genocide by his country's judicial system

An internationally recognized advocate for women who have experienced sexual violence, Mendez was the only woman member of the delegation to sign the Peace Accords ending the war. Her actions in holding out for gender equality in the agreements made significant strides for the women of her country. I interviewed her by Skype from her home in Guatemala and began by asking her about the effectiveness of women moving into peace processes and what more needs to be done.

"In order to involve women in decision-making for peace," she said, "it is necessary to strengthen affirmative action policies. The usual participants are men, who are not generally in favour of having women at the same negotiating table. Women are thus excluded from positions of leadership. For several years, I was the only woman at the peace table in Guatemala. Even though I knew women of quality, they could not attend. We had to push to change the format and go beyond just Party members. When we opened up the process to civil society, that created space for women. And then, with the addition of women, I found my own voice strengthened. It wasn't just me speaking."

She said she noticed a difference in the attitude of men following the Beijing Conference on Women, which dominated news around the world. "From this international source, local men started to think that having women play a role in building peace must be important. This enabled us to be heard on the fundamental issue that violence against women is a huge impediment to obtaining human security for everyone. The power imbalance of men and women and the removal of some barriers against women began to change."

Speaking gently, Mendez said she thought the UN could be a bit more proactive in including women on important delegations and missions. "As a former diplomat at the UN, I certainly agree with that statement," I said. "What more should the UN be doing?"

"I return to the subject of affirmative action," she said. "The UN should go out of its way to appoint qualified women, of whom there are many, to missions and talks in the peace process. The world must hear from more women who are given a mandate to speak and act. And men who are on these delegations need to be more attentive to the views of women. If the UN set such a standard, more nations would pay attention and start to do the same thing with their national appointments."

"SILOS OF THINKING"

The role of women in peace and development issues is a subject gradually coming to centre stage as political machinery everywhere wrestles with how to further reduce violence around the world. It used to be that violence against women was considered a private matter and not a human rights issue of concern to the international community. Now the prohibitions against such violence have been codified and written into international and regional treaties. Women are clearly gaining strength in the determination of their own lives. A consequential step should be the strength women can bring to the peace process, but as I read through the transcript of a meeting the UN Human Rights Council devoted to this issue, it became clear that gender discrimination still holds back women's participation. I was struck by a quote from Marilou McPhedran, who told the meeting, "As long as women are not key participants in decision-making, they will be vulnerable and marginalized by sexual and other forms of violence." McPhedran, an accomplished lawyer and human rights specialist widely recognized for her leadership in campaigning for gender equality protection in the Canadian constitution, is one of the most influential women in Canada. I phoned her in her office, where she directs the Institute for International Women's Rights at the University of Winnipeg's Global College.

"I'm deeply concerned about violence against women," I said, "but the attention paid to violence tends to obscure a basic development not just of women bettering their own condition but the more profound element of their contribution to the overall struggle to build the conditions for peace."

"You're bringing a sensitivity and an inclusive approach to this issue," she responded, "but, you know, Doug, you're not typical, with due respect to your gender. Men in privileged positions of authority are still resisting having women in decision-making positions. Gender-based analysis is not mainstream. The pattern of exclusion of women from full economic and political participation is still unmistakable. This attitude is nourishing the violence against women. It is women themselves who are trying to break the patterns of the past. The single most effective change agent in producing better global governance is independent feminist activism."

She dubbed male insensitivity to the role of women as "silos of thinking," by which she means that isolating women from mainstream decision-making on how the world should be run produces "silos of inaction" in bringing the thinking of women forward. "The damage is done by the silos of thinking."

"But hasn't there been a surge, even if insufficient, in placing more women in positions of authority so that women are beginning to play an effective role in issues of peace and development?" I asked. "I want to recognize the empowerment of women that has already taken place, so that we can have more of it. I believe that if there were more women in decision-making processes, our world would be a safer place with fewer wars."

"Yes," she responded. "I've been trying to increase women's leadership for four decades, but it's still problematic. I feel conflicted on this because the moment we talk about having more women in important fields, we introduce the subtext of not as many men getting these posts. And there's the additional subtext that only women know how to make peace." She recounted how Voice of Women, a Canadian anti-nuclear organization formed in 1960, debated whether to give two spaces to men on a delegation to the government. Some members resisted giving up precious space to men. But McPhedran argued and won her case for strategic thinking to produce a delegation with an alliance of women and men. "The integration of men and women working together in policy making is of critical importance. I'm teaching all the time that equality of opportunity is not enough. We have to have equality of results. This is lived rights."

A WOMAN UN SECRETARY-GENERAL

A new era of women's rights has clearly arrived. The "glass ceiling" is shattering. It augurs well for more political energy and finances to be devoted to building the conditions for peace. There can be no guarantee that more women in positions of authority will automatically produce a more peaceful world, but given the record of men in producing a culture of war over the past few centuries, the possibility if not the promise of a more feminine-inspired world order is dazzling.

Perhaps the most dramatic example of the breakthrough of women in world politics would be the election of a highly qualified woman as Secretary-General of the United Nations. This would have a profound effect on the whole dynamic of gender relations around the world.

The idea of a woman Secretary-General is certainly a live one as Ban Ki-moon completes the last years of his second five-year term. The election of a new UN head in 2015 will find the Security Council with a list of very competent women already working in senior positions at the UN: Helen Clark, sixty-three, former Prime Minister of New Zealand, who heads the mammoth United Nations Development Programme; Irina Bokova, sixty-one, former Bulgarian Foreign Minister, who is Director-General of UNESCO, perhaps the most prestigious of all the UN agencies; Angela Kane of Germany, sixty-five, former UN Under-Secretary-General for Management, who is the High Representative for Disarmament Affairs; Christine Lagarde, fifty-seven, a lawyer and first woman to be in charge of economic policy in France, who heads the International Monetary Fund. There are perhaps another dozen women in the UN system who have considerable experience, not to mention the scores of women who have served their countries in high political posts.

Geography plus political acceptability always plays a large part in such decisions. Despite the pool of strong women candidates, the choice might still be a man. Each of the five permanent members of the Security Council has a veto on the decision of which candidate's name goes forward to the General Assembly for voting. The political ascendance of Hillary Clinton as a strong candidate for the American presidency might be a positive factor in how the US government approaches this subject. If and when a woman becomes the United Nations leader, hopes will rise around the world that the present ascent of women will play a permanent role in peacemaking.

CHAPTER 8:
A New Generation's Expanding Minds

Since half of the world's population is under the age of thirty, it is evident that the mobilization of youth is critical to developing a culture of peace. The revolution in social communication among today's youth has been well documented, but is it leading a new generation to greater involvement in peace work? That's the question I put to Craig Kielburger, who, although he has just passed the age thirty mark, is one of the best-known "youth" figures in the world for his work since age twelve of helping children in developing countries.

"I agree that young people today have far greater access than ever before to the tools of information to create a more peaceful world," he said. "The challenge is to equip them with the ability to use the tools for social good and to cut through the noise."

To describe Kielburger as a whirlwind would understate the impact he has had in awakening countless young people to the suffering that exists around the world and what they can do about it. When he was twelve, Kielburger read a newspaper article about the murder of a twelve-year-old Pakistani boy who had spoken out against child labour. Incensed, he started an organization, Free the Children, to raise awareness about the exploitation of children. He journeyed to South Asia to meet child labourers and hear their stories first-hand. By the time he was sixteen, Kielburger had written a book on the subject. Free the Children blossomed and by 2013 had become an international charity and educational partner, with more than 1.7 million youth involved in innovative education and development programs in forty-five countries. When Keilburger appeared on *The Oprah Winfrey Show*, Winfrey donated $200,000 to his school-building program, which has built 650 schools and classrooms in destitute areas of Kenya, Sierra Leone, and Haiti among many other countries. Hollywood stars Mia Farrow and Martin Sheen are among the programs' celebrity ambassadors. Working with his brother, Marc, a spin-off movement, Me to We, gathers throngs of students to "We Day": well-publicized, stadium-sized events in major cities in Canada and the US. The Kielburgers attract marquee names, such as the Dalai Lama, Al Gore, and Mikhail Gorbachev to these televised events. The brothers also write a syndicated newspaper column inspiring youth to get involved in their communities.

In our phone conversation, Kielburger described an experience he had with the Dalai Lama, who had gathered thirty individuals for a week to discuss the greatest challenge facing the world, including such issues as hunger, peace in the Middle East, and nuclear disarmament. "We concluded that the single greatest challenge facing the world is that we are raising a generation of passive bystanders," he said. "At the root of our inaction and lack of political will to solve the big questions, we found that it often comes down to how we raise young people, to give them not just reading, writing and arithmetic but also compassion and courage, and ground that in a sense of community. The challenge for young people today is also a challenge for educators and parents and political leaders and for society as a whole to ask: How do we raise a generation to be engaged, caring, compassionate, and how do we leverage our school systems to produce people who care about a more inclusive, peaceful, loving world? We sometimes educate the mind too much to the detriment of the heart."

"Where do you think this leverage is taking hold?" I asked.

"I'll answer personally," he said. "This year, We Day has more than 160,000 students from over five thousand schools earning their way to attend our events in twelve cities across Canada, the US, and the UK. Over the past seven years, young people have heard from such speakers as former president Mikhail Gorbachev speaking about youth activism, and Magic Johnson on HIV/Aids and teamwork. These daylong events are streamed online. There's also a national broadcast that airs across Canada. We Day, with 3.3 million followers on Facebook, is one of the world's largest charitable causes on Facebook. Some five thousand schools and more than 1.7 million students now use Free The Children's resources, which help them learn about global and local issues, showing them how to fundraise for causes and to get engaged in service. Every week we send e-resources to teachers that make the curriculum come alive. We send these e-resources straight to the teachers' inboxes to empower them to teach about the world. We are just one of many organizations that leverage technology to involve students and their peers."

IMAGINE TWITTER DURING THE COLD WAR

I asked him if this galvanizing of young people shows up in the culture of peace issues, especially non-violence. "In the post-9/11 world that we live in, young people are hoping and searching for a culture of peace. Perhaps they did so in the past, but a young person today, living in the age of globalization, is growing up in a world where peace seems possible. Today young people are connecting electronically and through cheap travel with their peers around the world. This has incredible implications for young people. Imagine if Twitter and Facebook had existed during the

Cold War and young people on both sides had been able to connect with one another and bypass governments. Today that's
happening in extraordinary ways as we see in the Middle East
with the Arab Spring. This power is not always good, but we certainly have a new hope that, through technology, young people
will strive to create a more peaceful world."

"Yes," I responded, "but how will youth accomplish this if,
in so many regions, they shun the voting process and otherwise
express their lack of confidence that governments are the route
to better policies for peace?"

"I think young people today are shameless idealists who are
also cynics," he said, acknowledging the apparent contradiction
in terms. "Young people today care deeply about social issues,
they want to see change now, and therein lies the cynicism.
They feel the traditional institutions move too slowly and that
governments are not delivering on the promises they have made.
So they're impatient. They see their parents' retirement savings
eroding in the financial crisis and dim career prospects for themselves. I don't believe they don't care; they care immensely and
believe that if enough youth come together and create Facebook
pages, e-petitions, and rallies in the streets, as was done in Egypt,
they can topple a government and not have to wait four years for
the election process to take place or wait twenty or thirty or forty
years to reach a position of societal influence. That impatience is
why a lot of youth have pushed aside the traditional institutions.
Our challenge now is to help young people see that, in addition
to using modern technology and protesting, they must be part
of the political process. Social media has enabled young people
to state what they are against; the challenge is to organize them
to show what they are for. We've got to help them mature and
embrace traditional political processes and use them to move
forward. Likewise, the political institutions need to modernize to
speak to and be more responsive to young people and allow the

citizenry to have a greater voice. Neither young people nor the political institutions have yet figured out how to use technology to the greatest benefit."

Words seem to burst out of Kielburger without him drawing a breath. He's passionate and knowledgeable and I fully understood why he's such an effective public speaker. "You have this reputation for working 24/7 and going everywhere," I said, "but I want to present you as a human being, not just an automat constantly toiling. Tell me about your life."

"I define myself first and foremost as a proud, doting uncle," he said, referring to his brother Marc's eighteen-month-old daughter. Marc is currently doing development work in Kenya, and Craig said he would shortly depart to spend six weeks there. "I'm a great lover of Canada but also Africa. I've spent every summer since I was thirteen years old in Kenya. I'm on the road so much that my greatest pleasure has become books on tape. It's the only way I get a chance to read and keep up. I've got great friends in this work. We've stood together at marriages and funerals."

"Was it traumatic when you turned thirty and left youth behind?" I asked.

"That was easy," he said. "Turning eighteen was the tough part."

INTELLECTUALLY PREPARED FOR GLOBALIZATION

One of the characteristics of youth is that it disappears quickly and even Craig Kielburger is, by the rigorous laws of time, getting old. To see for myself how youth are responding to major world issues I set out in the fall of 2011 on a lecture tour of twenty-six Canadian universities. Overall I met about one thousand students in my seminars, where there was plenty of give-and-take. My subject was nuclear disarmament, but the discussions ranged over the main components of the peace agenda. Virtually all the students were born in the early 1990s, i.e., after the end of the Cold War. Not only were Hiroshima and Nagasaki just historical items, but the Soviet-US animosities and the policies of mutual assured destruction that so dominated the world agenda until the fall of the Berlin Wall in 1989 seemed relics from another age. Their level of knowledge of current events was not strikingly high, but what stood out was their curiosity, tolerance of uncertainty, and concern for justice.

The attitude of young people today — or at least the best of them, for their age group undoubtedly possesses its share of drifters — is one of holistic thinking. They understand much more intuitively than previous generations how war stops the human development process and, conversely, how democracy and a strong economic base ward off violent conflict. I found them challenging the systems of the world, particularly the political systems that so evidently do not deliver social justice. This generation, in short, is better prepared intellectually to deal with the interconnections of globalization than their parents, who have had, for the most part, to adapt from compartmentalized thinking to the multiple connections on the global canvas.

These were the findings I put before Paul Davidson, president and CEO of the Association of Universities and Colleges of Canada, which represents ninety-four Canadian institutions of higher learning. Davidson, who previously directed World University Service of Canada — an organization with a long record of fostering human development and global understanding through education and training — told me young people today see a "seamless continuum" between issues at home and abroad. "They've grown up in the post–Cold War years, have always known the Internet, and in many ways are more globally sophisticated than previous generations," he said. "They're coming to university with more intense questions."

"Can we expect from them a higher level of performance in

contributing to a culture of peace when they enter the mainstream?" I asked.

"The demands on young people are especially intense these
days," he said. "We expect them to have marketable and job-
ready skills, be involved in their communities, and be global
citizens, and to a large extent they are measuring up. I see a
significant level of volunteerism among students." He pointed to
the University of Guelph, whose students comprise the highest
level of volunteers in the whole city. The Guelph students run an
innovative refugee program, engaging with refugees while they
are still in camps in Kenya.

THE UN'S WORK IN PEACE EDUCATION

The United Nations has a long history of innovative education work. The UN University in Tokyo acts as a think tank for
research on development issues and is also a degree-granting
institution. The University for Peace, founded by the UN General
Assembly and located in Costa Rica, is mandated "to provide
humanity with an international institution of higher education
for peace with the aim of promoting among all human beings the
spirit of understanding, tolerance, and peaceful coexistence." The
UN's Cyberschoolbus, a global teaching and learning project for
students ages five to eighteen and their teachers, is a spectacular
example of online peace education.

In 2010, the UN launched a program to link institutions of
higher learning around the world with UN issues. Called Academic Impact, it quickly signed up eight hundred universities in
120 countries, which have undertaken to act on one UN activity
per year in such fields as human rights, global citizenship, peace
and conflict resolution, and intercultural dialogue. The Commission of the African Union and Fairleigh Dickinson University
in New Jersey collaborated to establish the Pan African University and African Research Centre. Anhui Normal University in

Wuhu, China, launched a green campus initiative. The Australian Technology Network of Universities initiated projects to stop cyber bullying in schools.

I stopped by to see Ramu Damodaran, the director of Academic Impact, in his UN office in New York. Damodaran, an experienced Indian diplomat who has also been editor of *UN Chronicle* — a UN quarterly publishing thoughtful pieces on human security issues — sees the UN reaching out in ways never achieved before. "Academic Impact is unique because we have been able to involve unlikely disciplines — chemistry, physics, biology, architecture, engineering — in carrying out UN themes. It's no longer the schools of international relations or political studies doing UN work. We've engaged the practical sciences. The essential premise of Academic Impact is that there is no area of scholarship, study, or research which cannot have a UN dimension." An offshoot organization, ASPIRE (Action by Students to Promote Innovation and Reform through Education), is dedicated to relief work in Haiti and other afflicted countries.

"Students have traditionally been vocal and strident on issues in which they feel a direct stake, but have little opportunity for direct involvement," Damodaran told me. "The Academic Impact offers the opportunity to match this fervour, energy, and urge for change in areas where they *can* make a difference — one activity, one research project, one fresh idea at a time."

BEYOND THE CLASSROOM

The number of universities and colleges offering peace studies programs has significantly increased in the past decade and this is another sign that those coming into positions of authority in the next two decades will have a higher level of understanding of the interrelationships of global problem-solving. Dedicated courses in such areas as the prevention of violence, conflict resolution, and sustainable development are producing future leaders better grounded in finding solutions to the problems that continue to plague humanity, such as the proliferation of nuclear weapons and climate change. If this higher intellectual awareness finds its way into the political processes, humanity will benefit.

Peace education, however, is a very general term and cannot be confined to any one set of studies or even to the academic world. It is at once a subject in its own right and a perspective infusing our attitude to the world around us. It belongs inside the traditional education system from nursery school to post-doctoral programs, but it also belongs in the community as a whole. Civil society organizations, often through their programs in the primary fields of international development, disarmament, environmental protection, and the advancement of human rights, are teaching peace as they go along. Participation in community life provides ways in which we learn about the world around us.

Though specialist knowledge is invaluable in conflict reso-lution, education is a very big subject that goes far beyond the classroom. Peace education needs to be put into a broad framework providing teaching encounters that draw out from people their desires for peace and provide them with non-violent alternatives for managing conflicts. A culture of peace is not a domain reserved for experts; rather, it comprises the universal attributes of truth, justice, love, and liberty. These qualities are at the heart of a culture of peace, in which understanding, tol-erance, and solidarity replace the constant concept of enemy, which a culture of war epitomizes.

The pioneering work for a culture of peace was done by the United Nations Educational, Scientific and Cultural Organ-ization (UNESCO), established in the first days of the UN to promote international collaboration for peace through educa-tion, science, and culture and to foster universal respect for justice, the rule of law, human rights, and fundamental freedoms. The opening lines of the UNESCO Constitution have become famous: "Since wars begin in the minds of men, it is in the minds of men that the defences of peace must be constructed." Though the exclusive, gendered language of the time might today suggest an archaic institution, it is anything but, and UNESCO is in fact headed by a dynamic woman, Irina Bokova. Her leadership is giving a twenty-first-century look to UNESCO's core beliefs that political and economic agreements are not enough to build a lasting peace; rather, peace must be established on the basis of humanity's moral and intellectual strength and cohesiveness. The agency conducts a host of education programs (particularly in developing countries) and intercultural dialogues, pursues scientific co-operation, and sets the standards for the protection of heritage sites. It's known as the "intellectual" agency of the UN.

Ordinarily, the heads of UN agencies are appointed by the Secretary-General, but the UNESCO Director-General is elected by the member states. In 2009, Bokova — who was born in 1952 in Sofia, Bulgaria, and served her country as a distinguished diplomat and a champion of European integration — found herself in an election battle with nine other candidates. She squeaked by on the fifth ballot. Some opponents criticized her attendance during the Cold War at the Moscow State Institute for International Relations, which supposedly made her a member of the communist elite. But that criticism seemed offset by her studies also at the University of Maryland and the John F. Kennedy School of Government at Harvard. The New York Times supported her candidacy on the grounds that "She played an active role in Bulgaria's political transformation from Soviet satellite to European Union member. That should be a strong asset in leading an organization badly buffeted in the past by ideological storms." When her first term expired in 2013, she was unchallenged for re-election. Bokova, who speaks English, French, Spanish, and Russian, is a passionate advocate of education for the poorest.

"Why do we still have more than 60 million primary-age

children and another 71 million adolescents out of school?" she demanded on the eve of a high-powered meeting in 2013 between the heads of UN agencies, the World Bank, and donor countries. UNESCO's research, she said, shows that $26 billion is needed annually to achieve good quality basic education for all by 2015, but international aid is stagnating, with an average of only $3 billion allocated to low-income countries for basic education. This has to be reversed. "Governments in poor countries cannot fill the funding gap on their own. There are plenty of inspiring examples to follow. In Bangladesh, solar-powered floating schools provide education for communities displaced by flood or rising seas-levels. Ethiopia and Kenya are experimenting with mobile schools that follow pastoralist communities, with teachers providing lessons when children are not herding."

UNESCO AND THE CULTURE OF PEACE

A challenging line in one of her speeches caught my attention: "Education cannot remain the poor cousin of international efforts to manage conflicts." UNESCO's position is clear, she said. "Education brings sustainability to development. It is a source of dignity and of innovation. These are the foundations for resilient societies and healthy states."

Bokova's office is in Paris and I sought her out for some elaboration in an email exchange.

"In all international peace-building efforts," she told me, "we need to strengthen and mobilize educational responses to develop new agents for peace and place them at the heart of international action. The goal of UNESCO's education programmes and partnerships is to develop comprehensive systems of education that embrace the values of human rights, intercultural understanding, and tolerance."

"How does UNESCO take forward the concepts of a culture of peace and the right to peace?" I asked.

"We work with countries and their societies across the world, at all levels of development, in both situations of peace and those of tension," she said. "Everywhere we work, the demand for UNESCO is high because, I believe, people understand instinctively the nature of a culture of peace, founded on the universal aspiration for respect, equal dignity, and human rights. For UNESCO, peace is a set of positive values, attitudes, and behaviours that place human dignity, respect for cultural diversity, democracy, and dialogue at the centre of social transformations. In this way, peace must be an everyday reality, an everyday experience and practice, led by individual women and men."

I pointed out that peace education can be viewed in two ways: first the basic education of youth in developing and fragile states, and second, helping youth everywhere, particularly in the developed world, to understand the practical elements of a culture of peace, including development, disarmament, environmental protection, and human rights. The success of UNESCO's work in the first area is measurable, I said, but how can we evaluate peace education in the developed world?

"Managing our diversity, learning to promote respect for our differences, and making diversity a source of strength is one of the greatest challenges facing education today," she responded. "We are seeing an increasing incidence of violence, bullying, and discrimination, both among youth and within schools. This stands as a major obstacle to building learning environments that are conducive to academic success and self-fulfillment. Peace education has to integrate these trends, together with the impact of exposure to a range of content on the Internet, as well as changing social fabrics and other factors. UNESCO encourages a 'whole school approach' in order to help learners gain the skills and attitudes to construct positive personal relationships.

"These attitudes are acquired day after day, in a whole range of contexts and situations. We encourage schools to integrate a human rights approach in all their activities, from teaching to counselling. We have developed a teachers' guide setting out action areas to stop violence in schools. Our Teaching Respect for All project, launched in partnership with the US and Brazil, is helping to address the challenge of living together by developing policy guidelines and teaching materials to help teachers combat prejudice, xenophobia, and racist and ethnic discrimination, and to support their efforts in teaching respect for human rights."

During the 1990s, when Federico Mayor of Spain headed it, UNESCO took a more aggressive stance in pushing the culture of peace agenda on states and even succeeded in establishing the International Decade for the Culture of Peace and Non-Violence (2001–2010). But, as I discussed in Chapter 5, there was a Western backlash against the suspicion, a valid one, that the political development of the culture of peace would lead to a claim to the right to peace. UNESCO has pulled back and now presents the case for a culture of peace in educational, not political, terms. Though political action by governments in progressing a culture of peace would be a welcome manifestation of their actual intent to build peace around the world, the educational grounding of the new realities of global living will build a stronger foundation to sustain future policies.

Bokova is right when she says, "Peace cannot be declared through political treaties or economic arrangements alone, it must be fostered first with individual men and women, with their communities, within and between societies." A rapprochement of cultures, in which people are helped to see the wholeness of humanity emerging from different backgrounds, is high on her programming list. Her goal is "to establish in the minds of people a global consciousness on the nature of peace."

Fulfilling its leitmotif that peace must begin in the minds of people, UNESCO wants to open up minds, especially those of youth, to the importance of peace and tolerance. Thus it advocates wide-ranging education programs to ensure that youth are educated in values, attitudes, modes of behaviour, and ways of life to enable them to resolve disputes peacefully and in a spirit of respect for human dignity and of tolerance and non-discrimination. The reality of globalization demands that the new generation understand that security cannot come from the barrel of a gun. A security defined in terms of human and ecological needs must replace the prevailing definition based on armaments, violent conflict, and war. Adjusting to the new security reality will not be easy, since the strategic interests of the major powers — fed by the military-industrial and scientific complexes — are still the driving forces in international relations.

Peace education offers a concrete strategy that goes beyond the current management approach to violent conflict. More than simply advocating against war, it seeks to create something more systemic and lasting from the bottom up. It aims to create the knowledge, skills, and attitudes that will allow people at all ages and levels to develop the behavioural changes needed to prevent the occurrence of violent conflict, resolve it peacefully, and create the social conditions conducive to peace.

Can learning to be tolerant, patient, compassionate, kind, and generous be evaluated? It's hard to quantify results, just as it is hard to show conclusively that a UN negotiation in a certain country averted a war. We know a fight when we see one, but it is hard to recognize peace. The essence of a culture of peace is mutual respect, understanding, and co-operation. These may seem amorphous, but they are the very qualities that lift up a society from the brutishness of conflict.

Some denigrate what is called "soft power" in international relations, as if the only thing that matters in dealing with the world community is the amount of weaponry a country possesses and the willingness to use it. Soft power relies on influence to achieve a just solution to a problem. It is an intangible and is frequently bowled over by the heavy tactics of the strong. But the powerful, so often using violence to achieve an end, do not invalidate the qualities of human concern for one another. Peace education is not flabby. It is a mind-expanding process preparing a new generation to live in a world where all human beings are interconnected.

CHAPTER 9:
The Virtual World of Peace

I started my working days as a journalist, and I loved what I called "fire-engine journalism": chasing ambulances, police cars, and errant politicians. But the glamour of the big-city newsrooms gradually paled when I began to tour the fragile areas of Africa, Asia, and Latin America and saw the vulnerable side of humanity, which, for the most part, is not white, Western, or Christian. How multi-ethnic humanity would get along in a shrinking world became a never-ending research project that led me into politics.

My long public career has led me to the conclusion that the mass media are missing the most important news story of our age: how huge numbers of people, truly "peacemakers," are struggling day by day to build new institutions for peace and human security that will affect all humanity. The media miss this because they constantly focus on selected violence. Often, knowing in advance that scenes of carnage will dominate what is shown on the screen, I hate to turn on the TV news. There's a maxim in the news business: "If it bleeds, it leads." The daily invocation of this chant by news editors is producing a public, at least in the Western world, that is indifferent when not cynical about the power of this transformative moment in history.

Like so many others caught up in the communications revolution, I turn to the alternate media on the Internet or the new social media for a broader perspective on the events of the day. It is only by getting beyond what the editors of the newspapers and TV and radio newscasts provide that I can get and hold onto a more balanced understanding of the world in change. But, of course, I have to be motivated to take the time to go to the Internet and find more illuminative material than the tip-of-the-iceberg violence chosen for me by editors who do not look at the world the way I do.

The ability to instantly access and transmit a wide flow of information in the new communications age undoubtedly opens up the possibility of a more peaceful world. An open communications infrastructure erodes some of the old barriers that led to warfare in the past, holds the potential to reduce the fears of unknown Others and better empathize with them, expands civil society networks, fosters government transparency to some degree, and vastly broadens access to education. Our interconnectedness, economic and social, is given tangible form. Real communication today soars beyond the old scenes of newsboys on the corner yelling "Extra! Extra!"

My criticism of the news business is laced with both nostalgia and affection for journalists today who themselves are struggling to cope with audiences whose character and wants are constantly evolving and technologies that are more baffling by the day. The news business is under a new kind of pressure, far greater than the demands of the next deadline. The Pew Research Center's *State of the News Media 2013* report found that newsroom staffs generally have been cut back 30 per cent since 2000. Cable channel news has been drastically scaled back and more time allocated to "infotainment" stories. *Time* magazine, which I used to buy as a boy because it explained the world better than anything else, is suffering a deep and steady decline in circulation.

"This adds up to a news industry that is more undermanned and unprepared to uncover stories, dig deep into emerging ones or to question information put into its hands," the Pew organization said. The public appears to be taking notice, for 31 per cent have deserted a traditional news outlet because it no longer provides the news and information they had grown accustomed to. Reading newspapers digitally has to some extent replaced the habit of print for a new generation, but newspapers cannot afford to keep giving their product away, especially with anaemic digital advertising. The *New York Times* is one of the few outlets making a success of its digital subscription program.

The turbulence in the newsrooms has unleashed criticism from within the industry. Tim Knight, media critic for the *Huffington Post*, rapped owners for "more and more super-easy-to-cover, super-cheap, super-meaningless stuff — crime, celebrities, disasters, weather and 'human interest,'" thus reducing modern journalism to "whimpers." He wrote: "The tiny (and getting smaller) group of rich and powerful media companies owning private broadcasters, newspapers and magazines increasingly have as their sole priority the making of the biggest possible profit in the shortest possible time."

To get a fresh personal view from experienced practitioners, I interviewed two of Canada's leading journalists and authors on how the public understands peace issues.

MEDIA HIGHLIGHTS "EXCEPTIONALISMS"

Doug Saunders, the thoughtful international-affairs columnist for the *Globe and Mail,* has on five occasions won the National Newspaper Award, Canada's equivalent of the Pulitzer Prize. Saunders, who was born in Hamilton, Ontario, in 1967, is also the author of *The Myth of the Muslim Tide,* which counters the politically charged idea, fostered after 9/11, that Islam promotes terrorism and Muslims are plotting to take over the West. We began our conversation with the contradictions of more information being available and yet little public involvement in the great issues affecting civilization.

"This is something that has always been the case," he said. "News presents us with exceptional events rather than grand sweeps of narrative or overarching trends. The most basic thing about news is the man-bites-dog rule. As a result, for example, journalists rarely write about Japan or Norway, peaceful places, except when there's something exceptional, like a tsunami or mass murder. You can expand this example of violence and conflict out into the wider world. Social media accelerates the pace. Now, rather than getting this exceptionalism on a day-to-day basis, you're getting it minute-by-minute. It creates the perception that things are much more explosive and violent than they actually are because it's the exceptionalisms that are being highlighted."

"What's that doing to public understanding of the key issues of development, disarmament, environmental protection, and human rights that define the human security agenda?" I asked.

"It's now much easier to understand those issues for those who seek them out," he responded. "But for the general public, the level of understanding is pretty poor. A lot of the cross-cultural barriers have been eliminated and that's good. On the other hand, a number of circumstances have made the large issues more difficult for the general public to comprehend. Large international projects that are not tied to some immediate outcome, such as programs to reduce carbon emissions, are difficult to grasp."

He added, "I think we're hardwired as a species to notice the moment-by-moment things and aren't good at discerning the larger trends. That is an element in human thinking that needs to be overcome. It's the responsibility of people in media and government to get beyond the moment and draw attention to the larger, more important trend lines."

Saunders drew my attention to one of the by-products of Twitter.

"Even though it's based on 140 characters per message, it's often used to send links to longer articles and essays that are coming back into fashion. It's now also possible to put out e-books more cheaply. So it's possible to go longer and deeper than previously."

The "golden age" of journalism is something of an illusion, he said. Journalism of the past was as obsessed with moment-by-moment events as it is today. The Watergate political scandal in the US opened up a period of a few years when serious political reporting was done, which in turn created the impression that journalism was an elite profession, not open to everyone. "But for a lot of technological reasons, the era of the journalist as the elite professional is no longer with us. There's a loss of the high seriousness of journalistic works that took months of research and were expensive to produce. On the other hand, we've returned to a norm from an earlier time and journalism is now seen not a cloistered profession but a reflective citizenship. Journalism is now something that everybody does to some extent and it's part of our day-to-day practice as a citizen. Facebook and Twitter have created the idea that the documenting of your world around you is part of your routine as a citizen."

We agreed that this trend might be called the "horizontal-ization of communication." "This holds great promise," he said. "While it has the undoubted risk of confirming each other's conspiracy theories and superficialities, it also has the potential for creating the sense that seeking out the documentation and narratives to explain the world is everyone's responsibility."

"LITTLE PUSHBACK AGAINST ESTABLISHMENT THINKING"

Linda McQuaig's books and her columns in the *Toronto Star* are trenchant social criticism that have earned her a badge from the right-wing *National Post* as "Canada's Michael Moore." Born in Toronto in 1951, she regularly jabs at the powerful in the political and financial worlds. Her latest book, *The Trouble With*

Billionaires, argues that the consolidation of extreme financial wealth challenges the very functioning of democracy. "What's your view of how the public understands the processes of peace in the world today?" I asked her in an interview.

"I think the public is rather ill-informed on these matters," she said. "I've always thought that the public is potentially interested and supportive of peace-oriented approaches, but is starved for information and even encouragement in thinking about these issues. In Canada the media reflects the dominant discourse set by the Harper government, and there's very little questioning of the government's military and climate change policies and how the government has moved away from UN-based solutions to world problems. The media has done little to be a check on power."

"Why is the media passive in conveying the complete picture on how the world gets to peace?" I asked.

"Well, we have to recognize that the media is mostly owned by private corporations, except for the Canadian Broadcasting Corporation. There's a tendency to go along with the prevailing view in the corporate sector. All this is part of a huge change that's taken place in society as a different paradigm has taken hold in which markets rule and government is bad and everyone is out for themselves. There's very little pushback from the media against this new establishment thinking."

She deplored the absence of media criticism of the "war on terror" brought on by 9/11 and the media's silence about Canada's pullback from UN peacekeeping efforts and the UN generally. The media deals insufficiently with global poverty, climate change, and nuclear disarmament, in her view. "There's so little attention paid to these serious issues by both governments and the media. People working for peace hardly get a mention in the mainstream media."

"There seems to be a dumbing down going on in both government and the media," I said.

"That dumbing down is almost a deliberate strategy to keep

ordinary people from taking part in the debate," she responded. "The build-up of the military is presented as a *fait accompli*. Public opinion is manipulated all the time. The media goes along with this."

"Who bears the greater responsibility, the government or the media, for the public's low level of understanding of the peace issues?" I asked.

"That's a good question," she said. "I firmly believe the role of the media is to be a check on power, not just a source of entertainment and fawning over celebrities and that sort of thing. There's always been an element of this in the media, but it does seem to be getting worse. The media is more focused than ever on a celebrity celebration culture."

I asked McQuaig for the reaction she gets when she writes on serious topics. "I get a lot of positive feedback, sometimes negative comments, but generally I find people interested in major issues," she replied. "I just don't know how wide the conversation goes."

"The level of understanding of global issues, low to begin with, is thwarted by the media's concentration on violence of all kinds," I said. "This not only discourages people but makes them cynical about the processes and mechanisms for peace. This translates into low public funding for the instruments of peace."

McQuaig agreed and said the mass media's attitude to violence is that it is inevitable. "We've lost that critical mentality that went into forming the United Nations on the idea that never again would we have the 'scourge of war' and everything must be done to prevent it. There seems now to be very little respect for the sanctity of international law, and the media does nothing to encourage respect for it. This is certainly impeding the development of a culture of peace."

"What about the relationship of social media to the traditional media?" I asked. "Which provides the stronger basis for forming public opinion?"

"I'm a big fan of the alternate and social media," she responded. "The Internet has opened up the world of information spectacularly. Social communication has added a whole new dimension to how we relate to one another. At the same time, it's very dangerous to assume that social media is necessarily bringing about the changes that we want. We become very caught up in it and connect with many like-minded people, but social media, exciting as it is, can give a false illusion that things are changing more than they are. It's an important tool, but the mainstream media is still very powerful in shaping the public agenda." She contrasted President Obama's mastery of social media in getting elected and re-elected with his difficulties once in office because of the intransigence of the political forces in Washington, which do not seem to be responsive to the desires of the people as expressed in social media. "The realities of power, where the traditional media are more influential, are quite restrictive. But who knows where social media is going."

THE DARK SIDE OF TECHNOLOGY

The new and wondrous communications technologies definitely have a dark side. They can provide demagogues with a powerful platform, enable new forms of warfare, or tighten control over populations by potentially oppressive governments. In Burma, for example, the extremist monk Ashin Wirathu (who calls himself the "Burmese bin Laden") uses Facebook to spread his message of ethnic hatred against the country's minority Rohingya population. In Iran, centrifuges at the Natanz nuclear enrichment facility were the subject of a physically destructive 2010 cyberattack apparently conducted by the United States and Israel, an act that some legal experts contend was likely an illegal "act of force," violating the UN charter. President Obama wondered aloud what would happen if American infrastructure was the target of a similar kind of attack. And in the United States itself, the National Security Agency (NSA) is already intercepting, collecting, and storing trillions of pieces of electronic information (e-mails, phone calls, Skype video calls, and more) en masse from its and the world's citizenry, in a process that constitutional scholars and privacy experts find alarming and undemocratic. Former NSA intelligence official William Binney, involved in the construction of one such surveillance system, warns that the mechanisms for a "turnkey totalitarian state" are already in place. Daniel Ellsberg, who leaked the Pentagon Papers, contends that an "executive coup" against the US constitution has already taken place. Clearly, the new communications technologies are capable of fostering tyranny as easily as they open up the world to all of us.

The digital dazzle, in its early stages, leaves something still incomplete about the communications revolution. The great debates over the future of humanity rarely engage the public, despite the access to vast amounts of information. What newspaper or mainstream TV station deals consistently with such core public issues as global co-operation for common survival, narrowing the gap between the rich and poor, the nuclear arms race, prevention of genocides, and the rule of law in conducting human affairs? Environmental damage, human rights violations, and the eruptions of peoples, all quite visual, are highlighted in the mass media, but the subtler story of individuals and groups daily assembling the new foundations for peace in a globalized world remains invisible. We run the very real risk of, as media theorist and cultural critic Neil Postman once put it, "amusing ourselves to death" with torrents of trivial information that distract us from deeper issues.

Can the Internet and social media uplift mainstream thinking? It may take some time to build the evidence.

Google executives Eric Schmidt and Jared Cohen, perched at the forefront of the communications revolution, admit in the first sentence of their book, *The New Digital Age*, "The Internet is among the few things humans have built that they don't truly understand." We understand that a small device held in the palm of our hand can bring us in an instant virtually every known fact in the universe. We understand that five billion people in the world are interconnected by cell phone transmission. We understand that we can flash the newest pictures of the family baby to 150 Facebook "friends" with a keystroke. But we don't yet understand how the new ability to interconnect with people of other cultures, religions, and races offers humanity the opportunity to free ourselves from the old chains of ignorance, bigotry, racism, and the other "isms" that have locked human minds for centuries.

We should not fall into the trap of equating technological progress with moral progress. The values of non-violence and global social justice, at the heart of a culture of peace, apply in judging both the traditional and the social media. It is not the "tools" of communication, old and new, that will make the world a more humane place but what the purveyors of those tools will do with them. The performance of the traditional media, still powerful in forming public opinion about peace issues, needs to be examined in light of the influence of the new social media.

A DISCONNECT IN UNDERSTANDING THE UN

Since I have been principally interested in how the communications revolution affects the prospects for a more peaceful world, I asked the UN's Under-Secretary-General for Communications how the United Nations gets its message out. Peter Launsky-Tiefenthal, a multilingual Austrian diplomat, is also Coordinator for Multilingualism, a challenging task, since the UN operates in six official languages — Arabic, Chinese, English, French, Russian, and Spanish — and reaches out in scores more tongues. "In addition to its websites and press releases, what is the approach you use to telling the world about the multifaceted work of the UN?"

I asked him in a Skype interview from his New York office.

"The new media lends itself to making every single UN employee a spokesperson," he said. "The time is long past when you could centralize the message. We make sure that messages go out in many languages in as close to real time as possible and do not contradict one another. We encourage colleagues to communicate in their own languages their work in helping refugees, administering vaccinations, delivering food supplies, and such activities. We do this in fifty-three languages and many more dialects. We're not just translating, but creating and producing material in these languages. We also find partners to help us. For example, we are partnering with more than 1,600 NGOs and more than a thousand academic institutions. The creative industry is also a good partner. There are, as we speak, thirty-eight film projects coming out of Hollywood, Bollywood, Nollywood (Nigeria). I'm going next week to China to see partners who have agreed to use UN content in their films, documentaries, and TV series."

He described how scriptwriters for an American TV series, *Revolution* — a post-apocalyptic science fiction drama that takes place fifteen years after the start of a worldwide blackout — sought out UN experts on sustainable energy to see how they could bring what the UN has learned into future episodes. Another popular TV show, a reality series called *The Amazing Race*, in which teams race around the world, interacting with local peoples, filmed one of its episodes on the UN site. The UN also uses celebrities to showcase its work. George Clooney, Michael Douglas, Yo-Yo Ma, Charlize Theron, and Stevie Wonder are just a few of the UN's Messengers for Peace.

"How do you think the UN's work is generally perceived by the public?" I asked.

"I think there is a general understanding and a great respect for the UN's humanitarian efforts, even though most people take this for granted," he said. "But there is a disconnect between the political processes in UN headquarters and the impact of those decisions on peoples' lives in many countries. We see it as our responsibility to re-establish the connection between the political decision-making in New York and the impact in the field."

Launsky-Tieffenthal helps journalists to "get out of Manhattan" and see for themselves what the UN is doing. He drew my attention to a 2011 poll by the Pew Research Center that showed that nearly six in ten agreed that the United States should co-operate with the United Nations, a more favourable rating than the UN used to enjoy in the US, which for years delayed paying its assessments. "Outside the United States, the sheer presence of the UN in their midst is viewed by many countries as a recognition of their role in the international community. We find more appreciation in these countries."

"When I go around the world," I said, "I see in most places a recognition that the UN is a very important instrument of foreign policy for the country concerned — except in the West — particularly in development. Why is it that outside the West the UN is perceived as an important instrument for human security?"

He responded that outside the West where the UN has a more hands-on and visible role, particularly in development, it is easier to grasp the importance of this work. The complexities of the diplomatic work on security questions do not find a ready audience in the West. The UN can only be as successful as its member states want it to be, and it should be remembered that the Western countries provide most of the financial resources for UN work. It would be "too cheap a shot" to blame the Western countries for the UN's perception problems, he said. All states must share with the UN in the task of getting the UN message out into the public.

EXAMPLES OF MODERN COMMUNICATIONS

In this new communications era, much of the activity on social media arises spontaneously from the actions of thousands or millions of disparate people acting in a loosely co-ordinated fashion on platforms such as Twitter and Facebook; this spontaneity (and the relative newness of the medium) is part of the reason future directions are difficult to predict.

There are, however, inspired people and organizations actively trying to direct social media development towards positive ends. Typically, these try to connect the vitality of social media's "bottom-up" grass-roots involvement with the focus and resources of traditional "top-down" institutional structures, such as the various agencies of the United Nations, non-governmental organizations, or academic think tanks. I take a look at four such examples here.

- *The ICT4Peace Foundation (ict4peace.org)*, working together with several UN entities, "champions the use of [information and communications technologies] for crisis management, humanitarian aid and peacebuilding." Among its successes are a collaborative tool that was used to carry out election monitoring in Egypt (2010) and Tunisia (2011) and user-editable websites ("wikis") that facilitated information sharing across humanitarian organizations and policymakers during the Haiti and Chile earthquakes, the Deepwater Horizon oil spill in the Gulf of Mexico, the Pakistan floods, and the riots in South Kyrgyzstan. Projects of this nature demonstrate the potential of social media to augment the existing institutional peacebuilding mechanisms by better integrating information from stakeholders on the ground.

- *Global Voices Online (globalvoicesonline.org)* is a community of more than seven hundred authors and six hundred translators around the world who work together to collate reportage with an emphasis on voices that are not ordinarily heard in international mainstream media. Arising out of Harvard's Berkman Center for Internet and Society, it is headed by former CNN correspondent Rebecca McKinnon. Media projects of this sort cannot yet compete with giants such as CNN or the BBC in terms of viewership — it is much harder to make development issues in Madagascar relevant to a general audience than, say, local crime stories — but Global Voices Online already has sixty thousand followers on Twitter, and the combined reach of sites of this kind is likely significant. The very existence of such media outlets shows that supply of meaningful, cross-cultural information can more than meet demand.

- *MY World (myworld2015.org)* is a global survey of citizens led by the United Nations that aims to capture the priorities of millions of people across scores of countries and render them visible in the form of an instantly viewable chart that can be sorted according to country, gender, and/or age group. Here people can gain a realistic sense of what their fellow citizens' priorities really are, nationally and globally.

- *VisionOfHumanity.org*, an initiative of the Institute for Economics and Peace, tackles the problem of making masses of information critical to peacebuilding comprehendible and relevant to a wide swath of society. It publishes a Global Peace Index, measuring "peace according to 22 qualitative and quantitative indicators" in the form of vivid, interactive infographics and publicizes important news stories pertaining to peacebuilding that generally escape the mainstream media.

Though there is no guarantee that modern communications will produce a more peaceful world, the trend line towards greater interconnectedness throughout the world is an extremely positive development. In *The New Digital Age* Schmidt and Cohen write, "The new level of visibility that perpetrators of violence face in a connected world and all that it portends will greatly weaken any incentives for violent action and alter the calculus of political will to commit crimes as well as to stop them." That is certainly a step forward, but will the collective power of the online world serve as a new deterrent to war? Schmidt and Cohen do not appear optimistic, arguing that violent conflict will remain a part of human society for generations to come even if technological changes alter the form of combat.

Drone warfare, which we examined in Chapter 1, owes its capabilities to the superlatives in digital communication. Cyberwarfare, in which an attacker can wreak havoc on a state's communications system, thus dismantling the electricity and transportation grids, is already with us. It's easier for terrorists to cripple a state's infrastructure with computer skills than to acquire the materials for a nuclear bomb.

Humanity has always had, in one form or another, the weapons of war. What is new in our time is the technological capacity to communicate across all the old barriers. This gives humans a power we have never had before to, as Hammarskjöld said, seek peace through a state of living devoted to action. Connectivity will hold governments accountable. We are not likely to stumble into a war, as happened in 1914, or to have a tyrant intimidate peoples, as happened in 1939, or to have a government increase its military presence in an area by stealth, as happened in the Vietnam War. The Internet will give us all the data we need to build and sustain mechanisms for peace. The virtual world of peace can now be seen. Whether the physical world of peace will arrive depends on moral will and political leadership.

CHAPTER 10:
Leadership 2.0

Why is there no global treaty prohibiting nuclear weapons? Why do nations permit carbon emissions to such an extent that global warming causes increasing planetary environmental damage? Why do governments spend $1.7 trillion a year on arms, a fraction of which would educate and provide medical care for every child on earth? Why is the vast mineral wealth in the oceans beyond territorial limits not made the common property of all peoples, with economic benefits going to the poorest? Why is the United Nations, the one place where all states come together to sort out the world's problems, starved for funds?

Raising these questions brings us to the issue of political leadership or, rather, the dearth of it as the new globalized world tries to find a path to the peace that is now within our grasp — if we develop the institutions and mechanisms needed to support human security for all. The twenty-first century has brought us to a transformative moment in human society with a new ability to chart our own future. The power of this moment of high technology, instant information, knowledge of one another's cultures, and a developing international law is rife with a potential for human benefit greater than the

Industrial Revolution or the beginning of the agricultural age.

The transformative moment requires transformative leaders, those who can elevate us and provide the social change that satisfies the deep and authentic desires of people everywhere. We look for these in the political realm because it is elected politicians, for the most part, who make public policies and decide how public funds will be spent. Yet what we largely find are transactional leaders, where one thing or another is exchanged: low taxes for votes or subsidies for campaign contributions. Transforming leadership seeks to release the human potential now locked in ungratified needs and crushed expectations. Transactional leadership, on the other hand, appeals to base instincts. Even those few politicians who do aspire to transforming leadership are usually dissuaded from persistence by the incessant clamour of the next election, the results of which they instinctively know will depend on their skills at transactional leadership. Politicians do not trust the public. And the feeling appears to be mutual.

But the sources of leadership are changing. The character of the modern, horizontal world gives a new power to civil society, with thousands, perhaps hundred of thousands, of persons playing key leadership roles in diverse areas of human activity. Measuring leadership is not as simple as it once was, for the interweaving complexities of modern economic, social, and political problems all but rule out a singular intervention. In today's world co-operation has been elevated from a pleasant attribute to a necessity in the joint search for not only equitability but the survival of the planet itself. The 2012 Earth Summit, in which 178 governments participated along with 2,400 representatives of non-governmental organizations, demonstrated the interaction of people and governments at all levels necessary to deal with the massive problems of sustainable development.

I have spent many years in public service and am generally critical of the quality of political leadership needed to build a safer, more just world. But I have never run a government and never experienced for myself the countervailing pressures on the desk where the buck is supposed to stop. So I asked two former Canadian prime ministers from two different political parties to engage in conversation with me about their views of leadership on the peace issues.

PAUL MARTIN: GLOBAL INSTITUTIONS

When he was Canada's Finance Minister, the Right Honourable Paul Martin proposed the formation of the G20, a group of finance ministers and central bank governors from twenty major economies[*] as a forum for co-operation on the international financial system. After becoming Prime Minister in 2003, he suggested the G20 move to the government leaders' level and the organization now holds an annual summit. His tenure as prime minister was also notable for the health and Aboriginal accords he signed. After his defeat in 2006, Martin, a lawyer and businessman who was born in 1938, continued his global activities, working principally on African development issues. We began our phone conversation by talking about a chapter he had just written for *The Oxford Handbook of Modern Diplomacy*, in which he called for the G20 to become a "diplomatic steering committee" for the multipolar world. He made the suggestion, he said, because "as the world's population approaches nine billion, this small planet is going to require better management."

"I have to say that as I look around the world," I said, "I see political leadership not measuring up to the scope of the global problems, whether in climate change, nuclear weapons, or the whole question of the economic development of peoples. What

---

[*] The G20 is composed of Argentina, Australia, Brazil, Canada, China, European Union, France, Germany, India, Indonesia, Italy, Japan, Mexico, Russia, Saudi Arabia, South Africa, South Korea, Turkey, the United Kingdom, and the United States. They account for 84 per cent of world economic growth and have two-thirds of the world's population.

kind of political leadership do you see that makes a positive contribution to building the conditions for peace?"

He paused for a moment before saying the question was a good one. "Part of the problem we're facing at the present time is, while the world's leaders certainly participated in the creation of the United Nations in 1944 and its evolution since then, the overwhelming power of the United States was a critical factor. At its best, the US provided strong leadership, even sometimes wrongheaded as in the case of the Iraq war. This leadership became more manifest with the fall of the Soviet Union in the 1990s and through succeeding years to the onslaught of the global recession in 2008. With the absolute chaos of the Eurozone, arising out of the failure of the Europeans to create institutions to make the monetary union work, and the paralysis within the US Congress, we have not seen that kind of leadership in latter years. At the same time, the two most populous countries, China and India, have been resistant to the thought that they should provide any global leadership beyond their two countries. So what we've got is the economic powers paralyzed, although in the case of China this is changing. So there's a background to the weakness of global leadership, and I think that's where it lies."

Martin said that these circumstances were why he had advocated so strongly for the G20 to expand its economic leadership into the diplomatic arena. "In a world in which there is no longer a single dominant hegemon such as the United States, and in a world in which it's going to have to share power, not only with countries like China, but with large emerging and wealthy middle powers, such as Indonesia and Canada, you need a body in which leadership can coalesce. Even though the US is still powerful, it is not as dominant as before. Thus institutions which can facilitate leadership are required. In short, there is no longer a dominant economic and military power. You need a grouping of nations that can steer the global ship of state. In today's world, that's the G20."

"Since the G20 is moving into the political arena," I said, "is there a role for the organization in asserting itself to prevent wars, recognizing that the development agenda of countries suffers when war occurs?"

"Yes, very much," he said. "The G20 is not NATO. You're not going to have the G20 countries declaring war. Is there a role for them in the avoidance of war? Absolutely."

He digressed for a moment to express his concern at the failure of Canada to step forward at this pivotal moment in history. "Canada turning isolationist and turning inward could not be more counterproductive. If there was ever a time when a middle power like Canada, one that was not blighted by the recession, could play a strong role, it's now. In the past few years, we have missed a huge opportunity." I said I was also concerned, but was in this book writing about the world at large, especially since Canada represents less than one half of one per cent of the world's population.

We turned to the United Nations and my complaint that the vanishing political leadership in the world can be laid on the doorsteps of the five permanent members of the Security Council — the US, Russia, the UK, France, and China — and the irresponsible use of their veto power. Under the UN charter, I said, these countries hold the responsibility for peace and security in the world and are thus undermining the UN's potential. He responded that while the permanent members are important, we should look beyond them as well, especially to those with younger populations as they will play an increasingly important role.

"We have to expand our thinking beyond the Security Council's permanent members," he said. "For example, China is more involved in Africa than any other country. It understands this. Hegemonic leadership is not possible in today's world when it has become very important to be able to reach out to a wider number of countries. We're living in a world now when the little guys are getting bigger and the big guys are increasingly more constrained. When the hegemony disappears, there is no longer the capacity of exercising leadership without bringing others along with you. That's why I pushed for the G20."

I said that whether the Security Council permanent members are weak or not, they still possessed the power under the UN charter to authorize economic and military measures and to ensure peace and that's why their role is still so important. The world has frequently been held hostage by their unwillingness to exert their power collectively in a manner that the UN founders intended.

"But does it really make sense that veto power be held by the so-called victors of the Second World War?" he challenged me.

"It does not," I said, "but they cannot agree on the reform of the UN structure. Former Secretary-General Kofi Annan tried to no avail. Nothing's been done, so the UN labours on. It's a wonder the UN has been able to do as much as it has, despite the handicap the permanent members have given it."

Martin responded that because the formation of the permanent membership is so dated, it's not reasonable to expect that they will show the kind of leadership needed today and that they represent a different era.

"Well then," I asked, "is the UN capable today of leading the nations of the world on an agenda for peace?"

"Yes," he answered, "I believe it is. But it's a different configuration of nations that are going to do it. The United States and China are key, of course, but they cannot do it alone. Leadership will come from the nations that make up the G20. Today a nation's capacity to lead, and therefore its diplomacy, is very heavily governed by its economic circumstances. I don't think you can separate diplomatic capacity from economic capacity today."

I then asked him to evaluate the rise of civil society in leadership today and its participation in advancing the UN agenda.

"I believe civil society is incredibly important," he said. "It represents in many ways the conscience of the world. Often in the debates on issues, NGOs play the leading role. Civil society cannot exercise its influence on a level with sovereign governments, but it can do it through sovereign governments. NGOs are severely handicapped, of course, if their country ignores them, which many governments do, but in turn those governments are weakened by failing to grasp the importance of civil society. When I was finance minister, I never went to a governmental meeting without meeting on the side with civil society representatives."

"How would you summarize your feelings about political leadership in the world?" I asked.

He paused again. "Economic integration and the globalization of issues, such as climate change, technological advance, immigration, disease, all of which pay no attention to the borders between countries, have proceeded much faster than has the capacity of national governments to get their act together to deal with them. We are now going through a very slow adjustment by national governments to globalization. If there is a failure of leadership, it's because leaders are having difficulty in overcoming the boundaries of national borders. Thus we need global institutions to allow leadership to happen. Meanwhile, the overwhelming rise of social media is enabling people to communicate beyond their borders. This is the paradox. Governments allow themselves to be limited while their populations (at least the young) reach out to each other." He said the new challenge for national leaders is to respond to electorates who still have domestic concerns but have also acquired a global perspective.

KIM CAMPBELL: LEADERS NEED FOLLOWERS
In 1993, the Right Honourable Kim Campbell, having served as the first female Defence Minister of a NATO country, won

the leadership of the Progressive Conservative Party, became Canada's first female Prime Minister, and set out a series of governmental reforms that are in place to this day. Her personal popularity could not overcome antipathy to the government she inherited and the party went down to a stunning defeat in the fall elections. Campbell, a lawyer and academic who was born in 1947 in British Columbia, launched a post-politics career in which she served as Consul-General in Los Angeles and a lecturer at Harvard University. A founding member of the Club of Madrid — an independent organization of former heads of state and government whose main purpose is to strengthen democracy in the world — she also held the chair of the Council of Women World Leaders, a network of women who hold or have held the office of president or prime minister. She was also president of the International Women's Forum, a global organization of women of significant and diverse achievement. I spoke to her by Skype in New York just when she was preparing to give a lecture on leadership and governance at the University of Toronto, prior to heading for Canada's north as the public issues resource person on a *National Geographic* cruise called "Fabled Lands of the North."

"When I look at the issues you're raising," she said, "there's no question the world has come a long way. There's no fear of hegemonic states taking over. There are threats out there, like China's hacking. There are still threats by governments against their own people. The world's swords have certainly not been beaten into ploughshares. But there are no major threats to peace and security."

It's harder to be a leader these days with so many streams of intelligence and accountability to deal with, she said. Today's issues on peace and security are complex and often filled with ambiguities. There's no perfect formula for getting good leadership. She used President Obama's efforts to control nuclear proliferation as an example. Obama made a good start, but was thwarted by Congress. Perhaps Congress should have stopped President George W. Bush from going to war in Iraq; but Congress constraining Obama has been a setback. "I think President Obama will go down in history as a pretty good president, but will he be as good a president as he would like to have been? He's dealing with enormously difficult circumstances and it's the very structure a democracy puts in place to constrain excesses of leadership that we now see constraining necessary exercises of leadership."

Most leaders draw up a circle of confidants around them to decide how far the leader can move and still maintain the support of those who elected him or her, she said. Leadership that can take people to a new place is rare. Often people don't want to go to these higher places. "We idealize leaders who have done this, but it is somewhat unrealistic to say that leaders should be doing things and get out in front with no one following them. Nobody gets excited by compromise. So when we talk about leadership, we also have to talk about followership. I think there are people who are trying to be leaders in the new context where leadership is extremely difficult. Maybe we have an ideal of leadership which is unrealistic in terms of the challenges of the time. When we look back on what leaders have accomplished, then we can evaluate it."

This led the discussion, as it had with Paul Martin, into the role of civil society. "The most important role of civil society is to inform policymakers and help them get the best information," she said. "Once you're in office, you're living off your intellectual capital and often don't stay abreast. Also, a civil society role is to help educate the public and move public opinion along and create the dynamic for politicians to move forward. Civil society should play a role in partnership with policymakers and create the political space for them to pass laws and regulations.

It's a synergistic relationship. When progressive countries create good legislation, this helps to advance the global norm. Civil society must do this respectfully, making it possible for politicians, who are always worried about losing their seat in the next election, to act. If I lose my seat, the next person may well not do your bidding."

I noted that former leaders, once they are out of office, frequently take progressive positions on the human security policies that they shunned while in office. "Why is that?" I asked.

"Maybe because, although they held such views when in office, those views were not in the mainstream of their party," she replied. "Also, when they're out of office, they have time to learn and they're not constrained by the need to balance views within their party and pull people along. They can step outside of that circle. They can then do what we want leaders in office to do, to use their stature and articulate a leadership view designed to move people along but without the peril of having to win an election in the process. Leadership without power or accountability may be an important kind of leadership."

FORMER LEADERS: NEW STANDS

The work of the Inter-Action Council is a prime example of how former leaders exert their influence on global issues. Established in 1983 as an independent international organization to bring together statesmen who have held the highest office in their own countries, it concentrates on peace and security, world economic revitalization, and universal ethical standards. In 2011 it established a panel to come up with solutions "to avert a looming water crisis" in the Middle East and Africa, which will lose a quarter of their water supplies by 2025 due to climate change and population increase. Those who took part in the meeting included former US President Bill Clinton, former Mexican President Vicente Fox, and former Prime Ministers Yasuo Fukuda of Japan and Gro

Brundtland of Norway. Former Canadian Prime Minister Jean Chrétien and former Austrian Chancellor Franz Vranitzky co-chaired the meeting. The stands taken in 2011 were bold by the standards of many governments: Israel was rapped for expanding settlements in Palestinian territories and East Jerusalem and must comply with the restrictions set by the International Court of Justice; wealth around the world is increasingly concentrated in the hands of the few and a new development agenda must include universal health coverage; the use of nuclear weapons would constitute a crime against humanity and a comprehensive treaty should be promoted to eliminate nuclear weapons. The council wants dialogue and lots of it "among rivals and adversaries," particularly in the Middle East. It wants more money dedicated to helping refugees, financing development projects in fragile states, and meeting the Millennium Development Goal targets. If all current governments moved in this direction, human security would take a big leap forward.

For many years, the council has been promoting a Universal Declaration of Human Responsibilities as a complementary and supporting addition to the Universal Declaration of Human Rights. The new declaration would provide an ethical base for a new social order based on the belief that freedom and rights must be balanced with responsibility. "A better social order both nationally and internationally cannot be achieved by laws, prescriptions and conventions alone, but needs a global ethic. Human aspirations for progress can only be realized by agreed values and standards applying to all people and institutions at all times." The council sees the new declaration as "a means of reconciling ideologies, beliefs and political views that were deemed antagonistic in the past."

The Inter-Action Council's approach clearly falls in the ambit of a culture of peace. It is political thinking at its best. The cynically inclined will no doubt dismiss it, but the experience of these elder statesmen, recognizing some of the key components of an agenda for peace, provides a basis of hope for those who have become disenchanted with governments. We return to the question: Why didn't these leaders do these things when they had the opportunity? Leaving aside the obvious point that election does not confer wisdom, let alone courage, on a leader, the answer lies chiefly in the constraints all leaders feel when they walk into their offices. Governments deal chiefly with the management of ongoing problems and fresh crises, not projecting long-term vision. It is therefore folly to put our hopes for peace and security in the world in the active political leadership of our times. The best of the leadership of the UN and the G20 and other new international institutions is desperately needed and should be praised, but it isn't enough to create the momentum towards peace that is possible at this new moment in history. Leadership beyond government is vital.

The great accomplishments of modern history — for example, Gandhi ending British colonialism in India or Martin Luther King promoting civil rights in the United States — resulted from extra-governmental pressure. Governments by themselves did not decide to free colonial peoples, stop discriminating against blacks, or free slaves. Great social movements created the pressure on governments that forced them to act. It is no different today in dealing with the global issues of nuclear disarmament, environmental protection, ending mass poverty, and ensuring the implementation of human rights for all. Governments must be pushed on all these fronts.

THE ROLE OF PARLIAMENTARIANS

In my early years in Parliament in the 1970s, I felt that being a legislator supporting or opposing government policies was too limiting in the face of the emerging global crises of the nuclear arms race and mass poverty. Why didn't parliamentarians use their access to governments to press them to initiate new human security measures? Some of my colleagues, including David MacDonald, Mark MacGuigan, and Walter Mclean, felt the same way, and so did a number of legislators in parliaments around the world I had gotten to know. At a meeting in London in 1980 that brought together about twenty legislators from several parliaments I was elected international chairman of the fledgling Parliamentarians for World Order (in later years, the name was changed to Parliamentarians for Global Action) and we began campaigning in our parliaments for measures to stop the nuclear arms race and end the worst forms of poverty. I led delegations to Moscow and Washington to plead with the superpowers of the day to take serious steps toward nuclear disarmament, and our work led to the formation of the Six-Nation Initiative. This was a co-operative effort by the leaders of India, Mexico, Argentina, Sweden, Greece, and Tanzania, who held summit meetings urging the nuclear powers to halt production of their nuclear stocks and begin substantial reductions. Former Soviet President Mikhail Gorbachev later said the Six-Nation Initiative was a key factor in the achievement of the 1987 Intermediate Nuclear Forces Treaty, which eliminated a whole class of medium-range nuclear missiles.

Parliamentarians for Global Action developed into a network of one thousand parliamentarians in 130 countries and branched out on an expanded list of global issues, such as fostering democracy, conflict prevention and management, international law and human rights, population, and environment. The organization was responsible for getting the negotiations started for the Comprehensive Test Ban Treaty and supplied the muscle to get many governments to sign on to the International Criminal Court and the Arms Trade Treaty. Its present leader is Ross Robertson, a long-serving Labour Member of Parliament and Assistant Speaker in New Zealand, who was an industrial engineer before entering politics. I asked him in a Skype interview for his views on parliamentary leadership.

He pointed out that parliamentarians are well placed not only to lobby for new initiatives but to follow through on their implementation. In the case of the Arms Trade Treaty, getting governments to sign on was just a first step. "Parliamentarians are pushing for ratification, then the development of national legislation, and then a review process to make sure the legislation is being implemented. In all these stages, the role of MPs is crucial," he said. "I see backbench MPs holding governments in many countries to account. Often they don't recognize the strength of their own influence." Parliamentarians and civil society working together can be a powerful influence on governments, he added.

Robertson said parliamentarians could be more effective by concentrating their strength rather than by splitting into many different kinds of parliamentary associations. But this diversity simply shows the widely ranging interests of parliamentarians, only a fraction of whom are truly interested in global issues. In latter years, a new association of legislators, Parliamentary Network for Nuclear Non-Proliferation and Disarmament, attracted about eight hundred legislators in fifty-six countries and concentrates on nuclear weapons issues. It collaborated with the Inter-Parliamentary Union, a huge umbrella group of parliaments in 162 countries, in producing a handbook for parliamentarians explaining the non-proliferation and disarmament issues. This is a form of leadership that doesn't make headlines but is extremely effective. The development of associations like Parliamentarians for Global Action and Parliamentarians for Nuclear Non-Proliferation and Disarmament is contributing significantly to expanded political leadership.

The voice of parliamentarians may in the future become stronger if the Campaign for a United Nations Parliamentary

Assembly takes hold. The campaign hopes that some day citizens of all countries would be able to directly elect their representatives to sit in a new assembly at the UN and legislate global policies. This is not likely to happen until another stage of history, but a transitional step could be the selection of delegates from national parliaments, who would be empowered to sit in a new assembly at the UN and raise issues directly with the Security Council. The European Parliament, in which direct election of its 766 members takes place in the constituent countries, offers a precedent for a global parliamentary assembly.

But any development of a global legislative body will be vigorously fought by those opposed to the very idea of a global government. The development of global finance, trade, and political institutions is difficult enough to manage today without trying to create one government for the whole world. Whatever the possibilities of a global government in the distant future, the idea generates such an emotional reaction from today's ultra-nationalists that pursuing it would divert attention from what needs to be done today to lock in the gains that have been made on the peace agenda. It is global governance, not global government, that is essential at this moment in history. This is far more than a small distinction. Global governance calls for the cooperation of national governments on trans-border issues that are in the interests of all to solve. The best we can hope for is that national governments will use their sovereignty to join together on the implementation of policies to get rid of nuclear weapons, close the rich-poor gap, and stop global warming before further catastrophes happen. Parliamentarians can contribute mightily to this agenda from their present positions.

JODY WILLIAMS: AGENTS OF CHANGE

What counts in leadership is getting something done. By this standard, few could match but many should emulate Jody

Williams, the sparkplug behind the International Campaign to Ban Landmines, which, as we saw in Chapter 1, led to the Anti-Personnel Landmines Treaty. Born in 1950 in Brattleboro, Vermont, she was something of a scrapper with her siblings in her childhood, but her fighting spirit blossomed into strong feelings for social justice. Seeing the ravages of war in Nicaragua and El Salvador, where she worked at an NGO for eleven years, turned her into an activist determined to do something about the havoc wrought by landmines. Soon her email campaign attracted dozens then hundreds of concerned people. The campaign connected with the government of Canada and, in 1997, Williams was awarded the Nobel Peace Prize. I was attracted to a passage in her autobiography, *My Name Is Jody Williams*, in which she wrote, "Aggression, violence, and war are choices and not the inevitable fate of humans." I asked to interview her and we had an email exchange.

"Why do so many people doubt their own capacity to effect change?" I asked her. "Why are they so passive in the determination of their own fate on earth?"

"Perhaps for a variety of reasons," she said. "Probably primarily because getting along in life can be hard enough. Work, children, paying the bills — all that can overwhelm most. And then the multitudinous problems facing us all are overwhelming as well. Sometimes people feel that if they can't solve them all, why bother with one 'small' issue. We aren't educated to be agents of change. We aren't educated to be involved citizens in our countries and our world. I spend a lot of time when I speak trying to help people understand that all actions for positive change matter and that if each of us volunteered even a few hours a month working to resolve the problems we face, we truly would transform our planet."

I reminded her that she had once described civil society as "the new superpower" and asked if she still felt that way.

"Yes, I do," she replied. "It is demonstrated over and over again that when people come together, focus on a goal, and create and act on strategies for change, we can change our world. Look at the Mine Ban Treaty. And then the Cluster Munitions Convention. And the Arms Trade Treaty. And the work of people dedicated to stopping climate change."

"What is your overall assessment of the role women play in the political work to obtain economic and social development, disarmament, environmental protection, and implementation of human rights?" I asked.

She answered: "I fully believe that women are the glue that holds society together. We are still struggling the world over for the recognition of our full rights as human beings. The more the voices of women are heard and included in meaningful discussion about the future, the more balanced our societies will be. You can't disempower more than half the population of the world and expect balance and sustainable peace."

To strengthen women's rights around the world, in 2006, Williams founded the Nobel Women's Initiative, which regularly holds its own summits. Her sister laureates Shirin Ebadi of Iran, Rigoberto Menchu of Nicaragua, Betty Williams and Mairead Maguire of Ireland, along with the later additions of Aung San Suu Kyi of Mynamar, Leymah Gbowee of Liberia, and Tawakkol Karman of Yemen, present a formidable team. They define peace as "the commitment to equality and justice; a democratic world free of physical, economic, cultural, political, religious, sexual and environmental violence and the constant threat of these forms of violence against women — indeed against all of humanity." I asked her what impact the group had had on the world scene.

"Obviously I'm not the most objective person to answer this question. One thing I do know is that the mere fact that women recipients of the Nobel Peace Prize decided to come together to use our influence and access to spotlight and support the work of women around the world for sustainable peace with justice and equality has amazed and inspired women — and some men. I think it reinforces the conviction that women tend to join together in common cause to find solutions for us all. Not that women are perfect peace lovers, but we tend to think about things differently from men. My friends Archbishop Desmond Tutu and His Holiness the Dalai Lama have said many times, in essence, that men have been messing up the planet for millennia; it's time for them to step aside and let women clean up the mess and move us all forward toward a better world."

"You've had a lot of experience going around the world talking to all kinds of people about peace issues," I said. "What have you learned most of all needs to be done?"

"Education, education, and more education," she said. "And for me that means a broad-based education, not just science, math, and technology. There should be peace education, courses in conflict resolution, meaningful citizenship, etc., from the time kids begin school. You get what you train for. We need people to understand from the very beginning that if we want a different world, we have to stop glorifying violence and war and teach the elements of building sustainable peace."

SPUN BY A MILLION WEAVERS

While the injection of fresh political leadership on the world scene would be welcome, it is unlikely that a new dynamic figure would make much difference. To pine for some heroic statesman or stateswoman is to miss the point that the transformation of the old world disorder into a new world order can no longer be done at the top but involves the movement of peoples themselves who have decided to shape their own destiny.

Leadership and politicians are no longer synonymous, if they ever were. One does not want to disparage the importance of the

Secretary-General of the UN, the office of president or prime minister, the pope or any other authority figure in the world of politics or religion. Such figures have power and they may or may not be leaders. But the transformation of the world from structured enclaves into a swirling, interacting, instantly-responsive human community has changed the nature of leadership.

The source of leadership today is seen in the technological bonding of the world through science, communications, and transportation. The environmental, trading, and financial interdependencies that characterize life on the planet reveal the integralism of the human condition. In this new understanding of ourselves as one race of people, old differences start to be erased. A new consciousness of individual power starts to be formed, even in what appear to be mundane ways. There are teachers in classrooms elevating young people's understanding of global citizenship, community social workers responding to the distress of human breakdowns, social justice advocates working for a better distribution of the world's goods — all these are leaders strengthening the fabric of society. The texture of this new cloth must be spun by a million weavers; a master spinner will never connect all the pieces. Leadership today, a truly transforming leadership, is all around us.

When people in huge numbers start to exercise their new leadership and demand that the resources of the world be diverted from bloated military expenditures to meeting human security needs, we will have moved closer to the goals of peace.

CONCLUSION:
Reaching Out

If you believe that the greed, corruption, and hypocrisy so evident in world politics cannot be overcome, if you believe that humanity is perpetually fated for war, if you believe that the United Nations is just a talk shop and cannot accomplish much — you will probably not accept the main point of this book: The world as a whole now has the most hopeful prospect for peace in the last several centuries.

But if you examine new UN mechanisms to improve peace-keeping, peacebuilding, and international justice now laboriously being built, if you look at the record of a dozen countries, ranging from Rwanda to Cambodia, that suffered indescribable atrocities but are now at peace, if you meet the new leaders in a myriad of civil society organizations in the development, human rights, disarmament, and environment fields — you will experience the pull of history towards peace.

A golden moment in the human journey has arrived.

All the big themes that comprise social intercourse — health, education, commerce, science, energy, shipping, communications, transportation, law, women's rights — are expanding. The major countries — the US, the UK, Russia, China, France, India,

Brazil, Germany, Japan, South Africa, Iran — are at peace. A new generation is coming to maturity with an intuitive understanding of the meaning of human rights in a globalized world.

The biggest advance humanity has made, as the twenty-first century continues to develop, is the public's growing understanding that war is futile. The rationale and appetite for war are disappearing. That would have seemed impossible in the twentieth century, let alone the nineteenth. We are advancing as a species because we know more — about each other, the planet and ourselves. The public rejection of war as a means of resolving conflict, seen most recently in the question of military intervention in Syria, has enormous ramifications for how society will conduct its affairs. The Responsibility to Protect doctrine is undergoing new analyses to determine the circumstances when it can be properly used to save lives.

I am not predicting global harmony. The tentacles of the military-industrial complex are still strong. Too much political leadership is pusillanimous. Local crises have a way of becoming catastrophic. The future cannot be predicted. We have lost opportunities before — notably the singular moment when the Berlin Wall fell and the Cold War ended — moments that prescient leaders could have seized on and begun to build the structures for a new world order. But I am saying that the world, soured on the wars of Afghanistan and Iraq, has finally righted itself and is on course to make inter-state wars a relic of the past.

Two factors are producing better prospects for world peace: accountability and prevention. We never used to hear much about governments accounting to publics for their actions on the great questions of war and peace. Now, with the spread of human rights, empowered civil society activists are holding their governments accountable for participation in the global strategies for human development. These global strategies, apparent in diverse fields from genocide prevention to the involvement of women in mediation projects, foster the prevention of conflict. Navi Pillay, UN High Commissioner for Human Rights, puts this gain succinctly: "Civil society everywhere is calling for meaningful participation, higher levels of accountability from governments and international institutions, an end to discrimination and exclusion, a better distribution of economic and political power, and protection of their rights under the rule of law."

There are many failures in building a culture of peace, but that ought not to obscure our vision of where humanity is heading. That vision is an enormous gain in the struggle for peace. But it is not enough. Organizing for peace is not one-stop shopping. We still have to deepen our understanding that development, peace, security, and human rights are all interlinked and mutually reinforcing. They are the foundations for collective security and well-being.

In the spirit of Dag Hammarskjöld, who held that action is necessary for peace, I suggest these seven steps — which are certainly not an exhaustive list — the international community could take to organize itself in an interlocking way to build the conditions for peace:

A Permanent UN Peacekeeping Force. Establishing a permanent UN peacekeeping force for quick deployment in emergency situations is hardly a new idea, since it was first proposed by UN Secretary-General Boutros Boutros-Ghali in his 1992 *Agenda for Peace.* The efficacy of UN peacekeeping has been proven through the years. Peacekeeping remains a critical element of a broader international peace and security architecture. The resources spent by the international community on UN peacekeeping are but a small fraction of global defence spending. But peacekeeping is done on an ad hoc basis. It often takes months, if not years, to assemble a force to respond to new aggression somewhere. A permanent, highly-trained, rapid-reaction force on stand-by basis is required for immediate deployment upon authorization by the Security Council. The concept of a "UN Standing Army" rankles the major powers, who fear a loss of their own dominance. Nonetheless, a UN emergency peace service (an international "911") would, if established, protect civilians and prevent regional conflicts from turning into wars.

Institutionalize the Responsibility to Protect. The responsibility of the international community to protect civilians from atrocities is starting to be better understood. Though still early, the Responsibility to Protect doctrine, which I described in Chapter 4, has a chequered track record. It worked reasonably well in Mali, the results are uncertain in the Great Lakes region of Africa, and it was misused in Libya. The international community should develop norms that can find widespread agreement in stopping human slaughters, and governments must put more resources into the prevention of such evils. The criteria for the use of Responsibility to Protect need to be sharpened. The principle of protecting people is firmly and globally established. It needs more time to become completely effective.

Nuclear Weapons Convention. It defies logic that the world has global treaties banning chemical and biological weapons but none banning nuclear weapons. With the nuclear powers modernizing their nuclear arsenals despite giving lip service to nuclear disarmament, we face permanency in nuclear weapons unless a Nuclear Weapons Convention or a framework of legal instruments outlaw the possession as well as use of these instruments of evil. Three-quarters of the countries of the world have voted at the UN to commence comprehensive negotiations, but the three Western nuclear powers — the US, the UK, and France — are adamantly opposed, while Russia will only participate when it is convinced the US will not attempt to maintain military superiority. All countries that profess to understand the "catastrophic humanitarian consequences" of nuclear weapons should engage in establishing the legal, political, and military requisites for a nuclear weapons–free world. The place to start is to hold the long-promised international conference on a Middle East zone free of nuclear weapons and other weapons of mass destruction.

UN Security Council Reform. Efforts to reform the Security Council have been made in the past but foundered. The fault lies not just with the five permanent members, which want to hog their power base, but with regional powers competing for permanent spaces on an enlarged council. The BRICS — Brazil, Russia, India, China, and South Africa — with their overarching new power should be recognized by the addition of Brazil, India, and South Africa. Germany and Japan would complete the enlarged Security Council.

Post-2015 Global Compact on Social Justice. UN Secretary-General Ban Ki-moon has warned, "The world is over-armed and peace is under-funded." The contrast between what the world spends on arms and what it spends on development remains a scandal. Nonetheless, the progress made by the Millennium Development Goals in lifting hundreds of millions of people out of poverty has led to some big thinking at the United Nations about how to eradicate extreme poverty, as we saw in Chapter 3. Persistent inequalities and struggles over scarce resources will plague all nations unless there is a global compact to deal with universal problems and advance social justice. Conflict, violence, and disaster are no longer marginal issues in global development discourse, and thus better mechanisms to reduce violence and foster sustainable peace are essential.

A Woman as UN Secretary-General. The environmental, trading, and financial interdependencies that characterize life on the planet reveal the integralism of the human condition. We live in a new moment. In short, we need a more human-centered leadership, and a highly qualified woman being selected to be the next Secretary-General would crystallize a shift in the world's values. There can be no guarantee that more women in positions of authority will automatically produce a more peaceful world, but given the record of men in producing a culture of war over the past few centuries, the possibility if not the promise of a more feminine-inspired world order is dazzling. If and when a woman becomes the United Nations leader, hopes will rise around the world that the present ascent of women will play a permanent role in peacemaking.

Peace Education for a Culture of Peace. Peace should be built into the fabric of society. This means moving the operational norms of modern life to respect for all life, rejection of violence, sharing with others, preservation of the planet, and acceptance of the common ground we all live on. The best if not the only way to bring this about is through education. The key peace education themes of co-operation, conflict resolution, non-violence, human rights, social justice, world resources, global environment, and multi-cultural understanding need to be taught throughout the traditional education system, from nursery school to post-doctoral programs. Although formal education is crucial, people learn at every stage of life. Vast amounts of material on the Internet and the programs of civil society organizations teach us the values of tolerance and respect for cultural, religious, and political diversity.

The culture of war is giving way to the culture of peace. That's worth a headline in any newspaper or TV newscast. You won't see such a headline, because the immediacy of existing violence trumps the long-range gains of humanity. But a global conscience is at work, stirring us, animating us, and making us reach out beyond ourselves. We must keep reaching and reaching.

ACKNOWLEDGEMENTS

It is impossible to thank everyone who has contributed to my thinking about peace issues over a lifetime in politics, diplomacy, and civil society activism. But I would like to express my appreciation specifically to the leaders from all walks of life whom I interviewed for this book. Their names are found in the List of Interviews on Page 202. They are an eclectic group: former prime ministers, former foreign ministers, Nobel Peace Prize laureates, senior UN officials, ambassadors, leading religious figures, outstanding women, authors, journalists, jurists, civil society activists — and even a prince. It was a privilege to be on the receiving end of their collective wisdom.

Fifteen years ago, I taught Khalid Yaqub at the University of Alberta and recognized his strong commitment to peace issues along with his high skills in computer technology and website creation. He was my research assistant for this book, providing new information and feedback in our discussions as the concept of the book evolved. He also gathered the information on the websites and films that are annotated in the Resources section.

I thank my publisher, Jim Lorimer, who has consistently supported my work. Other members of the Lorimer team, Kendra Martin, Jade Colbert, and Nicole Habib, made the book a better one. Meghan Collins designed a great cover.

I am also grateful to Ruth Bertelsen, my literary agent in earlier years, who gave me the confidence to proceed with the original concept of the book. She read the whole manuscript in draft form and gave me helpful suggestions for improvements.

For many years, I have benefitted from the wise counsel of Randy Rydell, Senior Political Affairs Officer in the UN Office of the High Representative for Disarmament Affairs. His knowledge of the UN is encyclopaedic.

Several experts in various fields read parts of the manuscript and offered valuable comments: Ken Epps of Project Plough-shares; Doug Cassels of the University of Notre Dame Hanna Grahn of the United Nations Development Programme; Fergus Watt of the World Federalist Movement, Canada; Bob Zuber of Global Action to Prevent War, New York; Bishop Remi De Roo, former Bishop of Victoria, BC; Peter Langille of the Centre for Global Studies, University of Victoria; and Marilou McPhedran of the University of Winnipeg's Global College. Any remaining errors in the book are, of course, my responsibility.

My friends in the Middle Powers Initiative have been a constant inspiration to me and I thank Tad Akiba, John Burroughs, Michael Christ, David Krieger, Jonathan Granoff, Alice Slater, Alyn Ware, Peter Weiss, and Jim Wurst. In Canada, the peace movement is enhanced by Adele Buckley, Robin Collins, Bev Delong, Walter Dorn, Debbie Grisdale, Cesar Jaramillo, Alexa McDonough, Ernie Regehr, Erika Simpson, and Murray Thomson to name but a few. Martin Duckworth, formerly of the National Film Board, helped me in the selection of films in the Resources section.

I also want to thank my assistants, Bonnie Payne in my professional life and Edel Maran in my household, for keeping my daily life organized and comfortable.

My friends laugh when I say that this book "will be my last." But, since I will turn eighty-five the year of publication, I am not planning to write more. I am content to depart the political scene with the observation about peace I made in the Conclusion: "A golden moment in the human journey has arrived." I call on a host of people, particularly young people, to develop in their writing and actions this golden moment.

— Douglas Roche
Edmonton, December 17, 2013

ABOUT THE AUTHOR

DOUGLAS ROCHE was Canada's Ambassador for Disarmament to the UN from 1984 to 1989, serving as Chairman of the UN Disarmament Committee in 1988. He is an author, parliamentarian, and diplomat, who has specialized throughout his forty-year public career in peace and human security issues. He lectures widely on peace and nuclear disarmament themes. Roche is the author of twenty-one books, including *How We Stopped Loving the Bomb* and *The Human Right to Peace*. He is an Officer of the Order of Canada. He lives in Edmonton.

LIST OF INTERVIEWS

The following interviews with specialists in a variety of fields were conducted in the research for this book.

1. June 16, 2012, Toronto: **John English**, author and historian
2. September 26, 2012, New York: **Bill Pace**, Director, World Federalist Movement-Institute for Global Policy
3. September 26, 2012, New York: **Bob Zuber**, Executive Director, Global Action to Prevent War
4. September 26, 2012, New York: **John Burrows**, Director, Lawyers Committee for Nuclear Policy
5. September 27, 2012, New York: **Ambassador Anwarul Chowdhury**, Former Under-Secretary-General, United Nations
6. October 9, 2012, New York: **Katherine Prizeman**, Global Action to Prevent War
7. October 9, 2012, New York: **Adama Dieng**, Director, United Nations Genocide Office
8. October 9, 2012, New York: **Rt. Hon. Helen Clark**, Administrator, United Nations Development Program
9. October 10, 2012, New York: **Margaret Novicki**, Chief, Communications Division, Department of Public Information, United Nations
10. October 10, 2012, New York: **Randy Rydell**, Policy Planning Office of Disarmament Affairs, United Nations
11. October 27, 2012, New York: **David Krieger**, Director, Nuclear Age Peace Foundation
12. October 31, 2012, New York: **Magdy Martinez-Soliman**, Deputy Director, Bureau of Development Policy, United Nations Development Program
13. November 14, 2012, Edmonton: **Steven Pinker**, author, *The Better Angels of Our Nature*

14. December 3, 2012, Ottawa: **Ambassador Biljana Gutic-Bjelica**, Embassy of Bosnia and Herzegovina

15. December 3, 2012, Ottawa: **Ambassador Edda Mukabagwiza**, Embassy of Rwanda

16. December 3, 2012, Ottawa: **Senator Roméo Dallaire**, former general, author

17. December 3, 2012, Ottawa: **Marie Gervais-Vidricaire**, Director General, Department of Foreign Affairs, Trade and Development

18. December 5, 2012, Ottawa: **Ernie Regehr**, former Executive Director, Project Ploughshares

19. December 5, 2012, Ottawa: **Kate White**, Executive Director, United Nations Association/Canada

20. December 14, 2012, Edmonton: **Andy Knight**, Director, Political Science Department, University of Alberta

21. April 8, 2013, Washington, D.C.: **Richard Ponzio**, US State Department and author, *Democratic Peace Building*

22. April 10, 2013, Washington, D.C.: **Mary Wareham**, Advocacy Director, Human Rights Watch

23. April 10, 2013, Washington, D.C.: **Cardinal Peter Turkson**, President, Pontifical Commission for Justice and Peace

24. April 11, 2013, New York: **Ramu Damodaran**, Editor-in-Chief, *The Chronicle*, United Nations

25. April 11, 2013, New York: **Ian Sinclair**, Director, United Nations Operations and Crisis Centre

26. April 12, 2013, New York: **Bob Zuber** and **Katherine Prizeman**, Global Action to Prevent War

27. April 12, 2013, New York: **Ray Acheson**, Director, Reaching Critical Will, Women's International League for Peace and Freedom

28. April 12, 2013, New York: **Jan Eliasson**, Deputy Secretary-General, United Nations

29. April 12, 2013, New York: **Anne Marie Goetz**, Chief Adviser, Peace and Security Section, UN Women

30. April 12, 2013, New York: **Daanish Masood**, Advisor — Political Affairs and Media, United Nations Alliance of Civilization

31. April 18, 2013, Edmonton (Skype): **Ken Epps**, Project Ploughshares, Waterloo

32. April 19, 2013, Edmonton (Skype): **Francesco Mancini**, Senior Policy Adviser, International Peace Institute, New York

33. April 19, 2013, Edmonton (Phone): **Lloyd Axworthy**, former Foreign Affairs Minister of Canada, Winnipeg

34. April 22, 2013, Notre Dame University, Indiana: **Carlos Villan Duran**, President, Spanish Society for International Human Rights Law

35. April 23, 2013, Notre Dame University, Indiana: **Robert Johansen**, former Director, Kroc Institute for International Peace Studies, Notre Dame University

36. April 24, 2013, Edmonton (Phone): **Ambassador Peter Woolcott** of Australia, President, United Nations Conference on the Arms Trade Treaty, Geneva

37. May 5, 2013, Edmonton (Skype): **Tad Akiba**, Chairman, Middle Powers Initiative, Hiroshima

38. May 7, 2013, Edmonton (Skype): **Beatrice Fihn**, Reaching Critical Will, Geneva

39. May 21, 2013, New York: **Leanne Smith**, Department of Peacekeeping Operations, United Nations

40. May 23, 2013, New York: **Father Jude Nnorom**, CSSp, Peace, Conflict Transformation Officer, Religions for Peace

41. May 23, 2013, New York: **Nassir Abdulaziz Al-Nasser**, United Nations High Representative for the Alliance of Civilizations

42. May 29, 2013, Ottawa: **Fergus Watt**, Executive Director, World Federalist Movement/Canada

43. June 5, 2013, Edmonton (Skype): **Judge Christopher Weeramantry**, former Vice President, International Court of Justice, Colombo, Sri Lanka

44. June 14, 2013, Edmonton (Skype): **Luz Mendez**, Vice President, Institute for Inclusive Security, Guatemala

45. June 18, 2013, Edmonton (Skype): **Peter Launsky-Tieffenthal**, New York, Under-Secretary General for Communications and Public information

46. June 27, 2013, Edmonton (Phone): **Leymah Gbowee**, civil society Activist and 2011 Nobel Peace Laureate, Monrovia, Liberia

47. July 2, 2013, Edmonton (Skype): **Prince Ghazi bin Muhammad**, co-founder, A Common Word, Amman, Jordan

48. July 3, 2013, Edmonton (Phone): **Craig Kielburger**, co-founder, Free the Children, Toronto

49. July 5, 2013, Edmonton (Phone): **Paul Davidson**, President and CEO, Association of Canadian Universities and Colleges in Canada, Ottawa

50. July 5, 2013, Edmonton (Skype): **Marilou McPhedran**, Principal, University of Manitoba Global College, Winnipeg

51. July 8, 2013, Edmonton (Phone): **Rt. Hon. Paul Martin**, 21st Prime Minister of Canada, Montreal

52. July 12, 2013, Edmonton (Phone): **Linda McQuaig**, Columnist, *Toronto Star* and author, Toronto

53. July 16, 2013, Edmonton (Phone): **Doug Saunders**, Columnist, *Globe and Mail* and author, Toronto

54. July 23, 2013, Edmonton (Skype): **Ross Robertson**, President, Parliamentarians for Global Action, Auckland, New Zealand

55. July 26, 2013, Edmonton (Skype): **Rt. Hon. Kim Campbell**, 19th Prime Minister of Canada, New York

56. July 30, 2013, Edmonton (Email): **Jody Williams**, civil society activist and 1997 Nobel Peace Prize laureate, Vermont

57. September 3, 2013, Edmonton (Email): **Gareth Williams**, Chancellor, Australian University and former Minister of Foreign Affairs, Australia, Melbourne

58. September 27, 2013, New York: **Jayantha Dhanapala**, former UN Under-Secretary-General for Disarmament Affairs, Colombo, Sri Lanka

59. October 7, 2013, Edmonton (Skype): **Ambassador Christian Guillermet** of Costa Rica, Geneva

60. October 8, 2013, Edmonton (Skype): **Nosizwe Lise Baqwa**, International Campaign Against Nuclear Weapons, Oslo

WEBSITES, BOOKS, AND FILM RESOURCES

Multiples sources of information are required to understand a topic as complicated as peace. In fact, there is so much information available in diverse sources that it is overwhelming. The place to start is the Internet. With it, I have been able to access rich sources of valuable information that are simply invisible in the mass media. Below is a list of websites which may help readers peer into a broader and more realistic view of the global community and connect with individuals and organizations working to improve the state of the world and bring about a culture of peace. The websites are followed by a selected list of books that I have drawn from and documentary films that I consider helpful. Of course, this is a personal list and it is by no means exhaustive. Others might choose different sources. But I have found these works stimulating and informative. They underlie the essential theme of my book: The world is moving, however grudgingly, toward peace and needs but the development of global institutions and a widening and committed civil society to achieve the goal.

WEBSITES

A COMMON WORD

www.acommonword.com

A Common Word is an ongoing, theologically rooted Muslim-Christian dialogue initiative involving hundreds of prominent Muslim and Christian leaders and organizations. This site, boasting half a million visits, features the founding "A Common Word" open letter, audio and video from associated conferences, and reading lists from Muslim and Christian scholars. The UN's World Interfaith Harmony Week (worldinterfaithharmonyweek.com) also grew out of this initiative.

CULTURE UNPLUGGED

www.cultureunplugged.com

This beautifully designed, privately owned website serves as an aggrega-tor of documentary films provided by socially conscious filmmakers from around the world. The films, ranging in length from a few minutes to over two hours, are helpfully categorized into themes such as "governance & politics," "peace & non-violence," "environment & ecology," "leadership & transformation," and "globalization." Several times a year, Culture Unplugged runs an online film festival based around one of these themes.

GLOBAL NETWORK OF WOMEN PEACEBUILDERS (GNWP)

www.gnwp.org

GNWP is a coalition of women's groups and other civil society organ-izations from Africa, Asia and the Pacific, South Asia, West Asia, Latin America, and Eastern and Western Europe. It aims to bridge the gap between policy discussions and implementation of UN Security Council resolutions on women in the peace and security domain. The website pri-marily documents past accomplishments in various local contexts across the globe, press releases, and solidarity statements. A more active presence can be found on its thousand-member-strong Twitter and Facebook pages.

GLOBAL ZERO

www.globalzero.org

Global Zero, the international movement for the elimination of all nuclear weapons, includes three hundred eminent world leaders and half a million citizens worldwide. The lively website features its step-by-step plan to elim-inate nuclear weapons, gateways to its international student movement with more than one hundred fifty campus chapters in twenty countries, and a preview of its compelling documentary film, *Countdown to Zero*. It has also a significant social media presence, with sixty-four hundred Twit-ter followers and thirty thousand Facebook members.

HUMAN RIGHTS WATCH (HRW)

www.hrw.org

HRW is one of the world's leading independent organizations dedicated to defending and protecting human rights. Ranging in focus — it covers arms, business, children's/women's/disability rights, migration and refugees, environment, counterterrorism, and torture — its rigorous investigations and targeted advocacy build intense pressure for action and raise the cost of human rights abuse. Its website, updated daily, provides a constant stream of news and briefings organized by date, region, and theme into a rich database. Its Twitter feed broadcasts daily to over eight hundred thousand followers.

INTERNATIONAL COALITION FOR THE RESPONSIBILITY TO PROTECT (ICRTOP)
www.responsibilitytoprotect.org

ICRtoP brings together NGOs from all regions of the world to further understanding of and strengthen consensus for the Responsibility to Protect (RtoP), pushing for strengthened capacities to prevent and halt genocide, war crimes, ethnic cleansing, and crimes against humanity. The website provides core documents for understanding RtoP, lists member NGOs, and provides links to its mailing list, twenty-five-hundred-member-strong Facebook group, and Twitter presence.

INTERNATIONAL CRISIS GROUP (ICG)
www.crisisgroup.org

Brussels-based International Crisis Group is an international, non-profit NGO aiming to prevent and resolve deadly conflict. It distinguishes itself through a combination of field-based analysis, practical policy prescriptions, and high-level advocacy, with key roles being played by former prime ministers and presidents and other leaders from politics, diplomacy, business, and the media. On its website, organized clearly by region and by publication type, the ICG publishes its monthly CrisisWatch bulletin, reports and briefings (roughly ninety a year), multilingual podcasts, and hundreds of newspaper-published opinion pieces authored by its associated experts. The site receives two million visits annually, and users can also follow the ICG on Twitter (alongside sixty thousand others) or its thirty-thousand-member-strong Facebook group.

INTERNATIONAL PHYSICIANS FOR THE PREVENTION OF NUCLEAR WAR (IPPNW)

www.ippnw.org

A recipient of the 1985 Nobel Peace Prize, IPPNW is a federation of national medical groups across sixty-two countries, representing medical professionals and concerned citizens seeking to create a more peaceful and secure world. Here you will find a regularly updated news and events section, publications, a series of blogs featuring reflections by members and running commentary from the organization's World Congress, and links to IPPNW's presence on a variety of social media sites, including Twitter (five thousand-plus followers) and Facebook (fifteen hundred-plus followers).

NOBEL WOMEN'S INITIATIVE

www.nobelwomensinitiative.org

The Nobel Women's Initiative was established in 2006 by six female Nobel Peace Prize laureates from four regions: Jody Williams, Shirin Ebadi, Wangari Maathai, Rigoberta Menchú Tum, Betty Williams, and Mairead Maguire. (Recent laureates Leymah Gbowee and Tawakkol Karman joined in 2012.) The website profiles the work of these women and others like them as they forge peace and justice and advance human rights. Visitors can keep abreast of activities by subscribing to the newsletter or follow along with nearly thirty thousand others on Twitter and Facebook.

NUCLEAR AGE PEACE FOUNDATION

www.wagingpeace.org

Founded in 1982, the Nuclear Age Peace Foundation is a non-profit international education and advocacy organization that conducts research and analysis on global peace and survival, supports the responsible use of science and technology, and strengthens the authority of the International Criminal Court. Its advisers include many Nobel Peace Prize laureates and it is recognized by the UN as a Peace Messenger Organization. The website provides access to research reports, an email newsletter, and helpful "Getting Started" resources for people new to disarmament and related peace issues.

UNITED NATIONS

www.un.org

The United Nations, through its various agencies, operates dozens of informative and useful websites around the world. The main site is a gateway to many of these resources. Here you will find an overview of the UN system, a news centre, the outputs of its main bodies (including the General Assembly, Security Council, and the International Court of Justice), statistical databases, the CyberSchoolBus colourfully providing materials, facts, and quizzes for teachers and students, and gateways to its vast resources on thematic issues: social development, international trade, women, energy, governance, and more.

UNITED NATIONS ALLIANCE OF CIVILIZATIONS

www.unaoc.org

In 2004, Spain and Turkey initiated the United Nations Alliance of Civilizations, institutionally dispelling the pessimistic vision of a "clash of civilizations." It now encompasses program areas in youth, media, education, and migration, aimed at improving relations across cultures and religions. Its outputs include a useful Global Expert Finder (theglobalexperts.org) that connects journalists to opinion leaders from around the world for analysis on complex political, religious, and social issues, a Youth Website (unaocyouth.org) that provides "a central point of reference for youth interested in advancing cross-cultural understanding," and a World Day for Cultural Diversity for Dialogue and Development campaign, featuring video contests and other ways for everyone to participate. More than thirteen thousand people subscribe to its group on Facebook.

UNITED NATIONS DEVELOPMENT PROGRAM HUMAN DEVELOPMENT REPORT

www.hdr.undp.org

The Human Development Report was first launched in 1990 with the simple yet massive goal of putting people at the centre of the development process. The website features the annual report itself, plus a range of data and visualization tools including country profiles, interactive graphics, a statistical world map generator, and even a "build your own index," which enables people to select and weigh health, education, income, inequality, poverty, and gender indicators of their choosing.

UNITED NATIONS EDUCATIONAL, SCIENTIFIC AND CULTURAL ORGANIZATION
en.unesco.org
UNESCO contributes to peace and security in the world by promoting collaboration among nations through education, science, culture, and communication. Its website is a well-developed resource organized around the themes of education, sustainable development, freedom of expression, and heritage preservation. It also boasts a substantial presence on Twitter (208,000 followers) and Facebook (132,000 followers), both updated multiple times a day.

BOOKS

ANNAN, KOFI (WITH NADER MOUSAVIZADEH). *INTERVENTIONS: A LIFE IN WAR AND PEACE*. NEW YORK: THE PENGUIN PRESS, 2012.
The seventh Secretary-General of the United Nations and Nobel Peace Prize laureate, Kofi Annan has written a memoir concentrating on his involvement in global statecraft over the past two decades. The terrorist attacks of September 11; the American invasions of Iraq and Afghanistan; the war between Israel, Hezbollah, and Lebanon; and the brutal conflicts of Somalia, Rwanda, and Bosnia all demanded political, not military, responses. How Annan tried to embed UN interventions in these tragedies makes engrossing reading.

ARMSTRONG, SALLY. *ASCENT OF WOMEN*. TORONTO: RANDOM HOUSE CANADA, 2013.
Women are the key to economic success and the means to ending conflict and violence around the world. That is the view of Sally Armstrong, Canadian author and activist, who writes, "From Kabul and Cairo to Cape Town and New York, women are claiming their space at home, at work and in the public square." In this fast-paced and lively account, Armstrong describes the perilous journey that has brought women to this point.

BELLER, KEN AND HEATHER CHASE. *GREAT PEACEMAKERS: TRUE STORIES FROM AROUND THE WORLD.* SEDONA, ARIZONA: LTS PRESS, 2008.

Here are fascinating portraits of twenty peacemakers, ranging from Mahatma Gandhi and Thich Nhat Hanh to Desmond Tutu and the Dalai Lama. The book has won many prizes for the inspirational stories it contains.

CLARK, JOE. *HOW WE LEAD: CANADA IN A CENTURY OF CHANGE.* TORONTO: RANDOM HOUSE CANADA, 2013.

The sixteenth prime minister of Canada, who later became an outstanding foreign minister, traces the qualities that made Canada a respected middle power after the Second World War. Canada is a society that genuinely respects cultural differences and successfully manages diversity. Recovering Canada's ability to lead is sorely needed in today's world, Clark writes.

DALLAIRE, ROMÉO (WITH BRENT BEARDSLEY). *SHAKE HANDS WITH THE DEVIL: THE FAILURE OF HUMANITY IN RWANDA.* TORONTO: VINTAGE CANADA, 2004.

It would be hard to find a military and political figure who has suffered more from the effects of genocide and knows more about what governments should do to prevent human slaughters than retired general and Senator Roméo Dallaire. Caught in the vortex of the Rwanda civil war and genocide in 1993, Dallaire was abandoned by the world powers as the wanton killing of eight hundred thousand Rwandans took place over one hundred days. His book is an indictment of how political establishments have failed humanity.

GITTINGS, JOHN. *THE GLORIOUS ART OF PEACE: FROM THE ILIAD TO IRAQ.* NEW YORK: OXFORD UNIVERSITY PRESS, 2012.

A journalist and scholar, Gittings is a joy to read as he traces the growth of the international movement for peace from the Enlightenment to the present day, assessing the inspirational roles of Tolstoy and Gandhi in advocating non-violence. Gittings argues that instead of being obsessed by fighting terrorism, the world should address nuclear proliferation, conflict and extremism, poverty and inequality, and climate change.

GOLDSTEIN, JOSHUA S. *WINNING THE WAR ON WAR: THE DECLINE OF ARMED CONFLICT WORLDWIDE*. TORONTO: PLUME, 2011.

Well researched and pungent, this study looks at the world's failures and successes in the struggle for peace and suggests that for the shocking idea that the world is becoming more peaceful to take hold "requires either a paradigm shift or at least a broken TV set." A scholar of international relations, Goldstein does not claim that the trend away from war is inevitable or irreversible, but "hope is an appropriate response to the world situation regarding war and peace."

GORE, AL. *THE FUTURE: SIX DRIVERS OF GLOBAL CHANGE*. NEW YORK: RANDOM HOUSE, 2013.

The former US Vice-President writes of the emerging forces that are shaping the world: economic globalization; worldwide digital communications; the power shift from the US to multiple emerging centres; unsustainable growth patterns; genomic, biotechnology, neuroscience, and life sciences revolutions; and transformation of energy systems, agriculture, transportation, and construction. Gore presents a sweeping examination of all the big issues humanity faces in the twenty-first century.

JOLLY, RICHARD, LOUIS EMMERIJ, AND THOMAS G. WEISS. *UN IDEAS THAT CHANGED THE WORLD.* BLOOMINGDALE AND INDIANAPOLIS: INDIANA UNIVERSITY PRESS, 2009.

If path-breaking ideas excite you, this book will not disappoint. In the capstone volume to the UN Intellectual History Project Series, three distinguished academics assess how the UN has fostered the ideas of sustainable economic development and human security. They write, "The integration . . . of peace, development, human rights and human security may be the most significant intellectual achievement of the world organization."

KENNEDY, PAUL. *THE PARLIAMENT OF MAN: THE PAST, PRESENT, AND FUTURE OF THE UNITED NATIONS*. TORONTO: HARPERCOLLINS, 2006.

There are many books on the United Nations; this one combines the historical elements that brought it into existence with the global reach of the organization. "When it works well," writes Paul Kennedy, the acclaimed author and scholar, "it is perhaps one of the highest expressions of our common humanity and a testimony to human progress." Kennedy describes the real UN: fallible, human-based, oftentimes dependent on the whims of powerful national governments . . . but utterly indispensable.

LIPSEY, ROGER. *HAMMARSKJÖLD: A LIFE.* ANN ARBOR: UNIVERSITY OF MICHIGAN PRESS, 2013.

The greatest of all UN secretaries-general, Dag Hammarskjöld is the only person to have been awarded the Nobel Peace Prize posthumously. His death in a plane crash in Africa in 1961 is still under investigation. Hammarskjöld remains a towering figure of the twentieth century. This new biography by the historian Roger Lipsey recounts how Hammarskjöld fused his spiritual insights and political instincts at a time when the UN's prestige was respected in national chancelleries.

MAHBUBANI, KISHORE. *THE GREAT CONVERGENCE: ASIA, THE WEST AND THE LOGIC OF ONE WORLD.* NEW YORK: PUBLIC AFFAIRS, 2013.

For Kishore Mahbubani — a Singapore diplomat, professor, and writer — hope is not just a wish but is grounded in reality. The world has changed more in the past thirty years than in the previous three hundred. "Never before in human history have so many people been lifted out of absolute poverty." He argues that the potential for a peaceful new global civilization is evolving before our eyes almost unnoticed. The West and Asia can successfully meet if the West pulls back from trying to dominate global institutions.

PINKER, STEVEN. *THE BETTER ANGELS OF OUR NATURE: WHY VIOLENCE HAS DECLINED.* TORONTO: VIKING, 2011.

The world of the past was much worse, argues Steven Pinker, Professor of Psychology at Harvard University, in this hotly debated and long (802-page) examination of the decline in violence in modern times. "Today we may be living in the most peaceable era in our species' existence," he writes in the opening page. Pinker challenges those who don't believe this with arguments and graphs galore. It's hard to be a sceptic at the end.

ROCHE, DOUGLAS. *THE HUMAN RIGHT TO PEACE.* TORONTO: NOVALIS, 2003.

"The peoples of our planet have a sacred right to peace." These words were inserted into the first paragraph of a UN Declaration on the Right of Peoples to Peace, adopted November 12, 1984. It became the basis of a book I wrote in 2003, outlining the development of the concept of a culture of peace and how this later led to efforts at the UN to have the idea of a right to peace take hold, not just be another aspirational document. The *Human Right to Peace* is the forerunner to my present book.

ROCHE, DOUGLAS. *HOW WE STOPPED LOVING THE BOMB.* TORONTO: LORIMER, 2011.

A worldwide movement to ban nuclear weapons has developed in the past few years. Three-quarters of the General Assembly at the United Nations have voted to commence negotiations. That's the positive side of this story. The negative is the recalcitrance of the major nuclear states to join this effort and the excuses the military-industrial complex still uses to justify continued production of nuclear weapons. This short work examines all the issues involved in getting from the nuclear mountain to nuclear zero.

SCHLOSSER, ERIC. *COMMAND AND CONTROL: NUCLEAR WEAPONS, THE DAMASCUS ACCIDENT, AND THE ILLUSION OF SAFETY.* NEW YORK: THE PENGUIN PRESS, 2013.

You won't feel any comfort that we are safe from the accidental detonation of nuclear weapons after reading the investigative journalist Eric Schlosser's account of the mismanagement of America's nuclear arsenal. Schlosser draws on recently declassified documents and interviews with military personnel to describe terrifying moments when a nuclear catastrophe was barely averted.

SCHMIDT, ERIC AND JARED COHEN. *THE NEW DIGITAL AGE: RESHAPING THE FUTURE OF PEOPLE, NATIONS AND BUSINESS.* LONDON: JOHN MURRAY, 2013.

The chief executives of Google have written a vivid examination of how "connectivity" is affecting how we live today, with continued advances in the communications revolution still to come. The physical civilization has developed over thousands of years; the virtual one is developing before our eyes. Schmidt and Cohen think the result will be a more egalitarian, transparent, and interesting world than we can even imagine. More peaceable? The tools are there.

SMITH, GRAEME. *THE DOGS ARE EATING THEM NOW: OUR WAR IN AFGHANISTAN.* TORONTO: ALFRED A KNOPF CANADA, 2013.

"We lost the war in southern Afghanistan and it broke my heart." These opening words in a trenchant account of the folly of the Afghan war reveal the passion and perspicacity of a great Canadian journalist. Graeme Smith cares deeply about the people of Afghanistan, who have suffered as a result of the West's miscalculations about warfare.

VAN RIET, ROB, AND ALYN WARE. *SUPPORTING NUCLEAR NON-PROLIFERATION AND DISARMAMENT: HANDBOOK FOR PARLIAMENTARIANS.* GENEVA: INTER-PARLIAMENTARY UNION, 2012.

Though this handbook was prepared by the Parliamentary Network for Nuclear Non-Proliferation and Disarmament for parliamentarians, I recommend it for general readership. The issues at the heart of the struggle to make the world nuclear weapons–free are concisely presented in an attractive format. Examples of good practice and recommendations for future political action are clearly set out.

WILLIAMS, JODY. *MY NAME IS JODY WILLIAMS: A VERMONT GIRL'S WINDING PATH TO THE NOBEL PEACE PRIZE.* BERKELEY: UNIVERSITY OF CALIFORNIA PRESS, 2013.

Her fans range from Archbishop Desmond Tutu to the actor and activist Mia Farrow. Jody Williams, who won the 1997 Nobel Peace Prize for her work to ban landmines, is a force of nature. From humble beginnings, she developed a powerful international team of activists who produced a result that has saved countless lives. Relentless and unyielding, Williams writes, "I've remained crystal clear that I am a grassroots activist to the core."

FILMS

IF YOU LOVE THIS PLANET (1982)

www.nfb.ca/film/if_you_love_this_planet

This classic short documentary produced by the National Film Board of Canada presents anti-nuclear activist Dr. Helen Caldicott's lecture on the danger of nuclear weapons. Despite being officially designated as "foreign political propaganda" by the US Department of Justice and suppressed in the United States, the film went on to win the 1982 Academy Award for Documentary Short Subject.

THE CENTURY OF THE SELF (2002) / *THE POWER OF NIGHTMARES: THE RISE OF THE POLITICS OF FEAR* (2004) / *THE TRAP: WHAT HAPPENED TO OUR DREAM OF FREEDOM* (2007)

www.topdocumentaryfilms.com/the-century-of-the-self

topdocumentaryfilms.com/the-trap

This trio of BBC documentaries by English filmmaker Adam Curtis provides a sweeping, illuminating insight into how influential theories, movements, and institutions have shaped Western democracies in recent history and over the past hundred years. *The Century of the Self* examines how Freud's theories and the public relations industry that spawned from them have been used by powerful interests in government and business to distort American and British democratic processes. *The Power of Nightmares* charts how progressive ideologies have given way over the past thirty-five years to a more managerial style of governance with the result that many politicians see little alternative to austere and militarist policies. Seemingly unable to provide a holistic and hopeful vision in a fragmented, competitive world, many politicians attain power by accentuating the fears of an insecure public. *The Trap* explores the concept and definition of freedom, charting "how a simplistic model of human beings as self-seeking, almost robotic, creatures led to today's [narrow] idea of freedom" and reveals how flaws in this model have became apparent over time — thus giving us a basis for a more humane model of society based on a more optimistic and accurate reflection of human nature.

HOTEL RWANDA (2004)

Widely Available on DVD

Hotel Rwanda is a hard-to-watch yet gripping Oscar-winning drama based on the story of hotelier Paul Rusesabagina, who saved twelve hundred refugees by granting them shelter at the Hôtel des Mille Collines during the 1994 Rwandan genocide. Focusing on the actions of two men who cannot rely on an indifferent international community — Rusesabagina and Colonel Oliver (based on Canadian Lieutenant-General Roméo Dallaire) — the film draws attention to how conscientious individuals must choose to function in an impossible situation. The film is listed by the American Film Institute as one of the one hundred most inspirational movies of all time.

LORD OF WAR (2005)

Widely Available on DVD

This feature film is a bleak comedy with a serious message, produced by and staring Nicholas Cage. Cage plays an international arms dealer who has "done business with every army but the Salvation Army" and takes viewers on a tour through the shadowy industry that turns twelve-year-olds into killers and seeds conflict worldwide. Amnesty International, the human rights organization, officially endorsed the film for highlighting the problem of arms trafficking by the international arms industry.

MAKING A KILLING: INSIDE THE INTERNATIONAL ARMS TRADE (2006)

www.youtube.com/watch?v=r0sC3CSp24E

In this fifteen-minute documentary, experts from Amnesty International, Human Rights Watch, the World Security Institute, and other organizations provide an overview of the history, scale, appalling nature, and composition of the international arms trade problem. Among many surprising details, viewers learn how lethal mines are sometimes disguised as children's toys and how the governments of the Security Council's permanent members — the United States, United Kingdom, Russia, France, and China — work hand-in-hand with arms dealers to market weapons that are used not only to kill innocent people but also in contexts that are against the interests of the merchant nations.

FINDING OUR VOICES: STORIES OF AMERICAN DISSENT (2008)

www.cultureunplugged.com/documentary/watch-online/play/11544/Finding-Our-Voices

Narrated by Martin Sheen, *Finding Our Voices* profiles eight diverse Americans who spoke out against the war in Iraq, risking their jobs, reputations, and even their freedom for the lives of soldiers and for those living in the Middle East. Blending four years of street footage and interviews, the film considers the role and effect of protest in today's democratic culture, and raises the question "If there is no dissent, and therefore no debate, do we still have a democracy?"

THE STRANGEST DREAM (2010)

www.nfb.ca/playlists/douglas-roche/strength-peace/

In a listing of films on peace issues I annotated for the National Film Board of Canada, the story of Joseph Rotblat stands out. Rotblat was the only nuclear scientist to leave the Manhattan Project, the US government's secret program to build the first atomic bomb. His decision was based on moral grounds. The film retraces the history of nuclear weapons, from the first test in New Mexico, to Hiroshima, where we see survivors of the first atomic attack. Branded a traitor and spy, Rotblat went from designing atomic bombs to researching the medical uses of radiation. Together with Bertrand Russell he helped create the modern peace movement, and eventually won the Nobel Peace Prize.

COUNTDOWN TO ZERO (2010)

www.countdowntozerofilm.com

This film takes viewers through the past, present, and possible future of nuclear weapons in the United States, Russia, the United Kingdom, and Pakistan. Oscar-winning filmmaker Lawrence Bender shows how the world's fragile nuclear balance could be shattered by an act of terrorism, failed diplomacy, or simple accident. This controversial film has inspired heated responses from both supporters and detractors of nuclear weapons.

UNDP'S ONE DAY ON EARTH (2012)

www.onedayonearth.org/page/films

On October 20, 2010, United Nations Development Programme staff members in more than one hundred countries each filmed their view of the daily operations of the UNDP. This film distills that copious footage into a feature-length documentary that vividly showcases the work the organization does to further women's empowerment, sustainable development, cultural diversity, and the Millennium Development Goals.

THE UNTOLD STORY: GLOBAL PEACEMAKING AND INTERRELIGIOUS COOPERATION (2012)

www.vimeo.com/52569810

This is a lecture by Dr. William F. Vendley, Secretary General of the World Conference for Religions and Peace (WCRP), speaking as part of the Rothko Chapel's programme on art, spirituality, and human rights. WCRP is the world's largest and most representative multi-religious coalition promoting common action among religious communities to prevent war, address poverty, and foster ecological stewardship. In this lecture, Dr. Vendley conveys stories of interreligious cooperation in contexts ranging from conflict resolution (Bosnia, Uganda) to pandemic management across the African continent to the crisis in Syria.

GRANNY POWER: THE FILM (2013)

www.grannypowerthefilm.com

This is a documentary about a very original international activist movement fighting for peace, social justice, and the environment: the Raging Grannies. With "disarming smiles, biting lyrics, flowery hats, and a gift for inventive, off-the-wall protest," they prove how "life can be lived to its fullest, in a meaningful way, to the end." The film details the founding of the movement, follows the lives of several of these witty and energetic women, and inspires people of all ages to get involved in making peace and justice a reality.

UN ASSOCIATION FILM FESTIVAL
www.unaff.org
The UN Film Festival takes place annually in the San Francisco Bay Area and features about seventy documentary films focusing on human rights, environmental themes, population migrations, women's rights, refugees, homelessness, racism, health, universal education, and war and peace. Highlights of the 2013 programme:

- *Citizen Koch* details the personal and political consequences of a broken electoral system through the stories of three Wisconsin state employees whose staunch Republican loyalty is challenged when Gov. Scott Walker moves to take away their union rights and simultaneously bestows tax breaks on large corporations.

- *The Revolutionary Optimist* is an inspiring story that follows Amlan, a lawyer/choreographer, and three of the children he works with in the slums of Kolkata. Together they embark on a journey through adolescence, as the children become change agents, overcoming poverty and transforming their neighbourhoods.

- *The Suffering Grasses* documents competing, still-evolving impulses among opponents of the Assad regime at the onset of the Syrian revolution and provides an intimate view of Syria's refugee crisis.

INDEX